Simple
Household
S lutions
for cleaning, cooking & more

everything **organized**

Simple Household Solutions
©Product Concept Mfg., Inc.

Simple Household Solutions
ISBN 978-0-9909508-1-3

Published by Product Concept Mfg., Inc.
2175 N. Academy Circle #200, Colorado Springs, CO 80909

©2014 Product Concept Mfg., Inc. All rights reserved.

Written and Compiled by Patricia Mitchell
in association with Product Concept Mfg., Inc.

Sayings not having a credit listed are contributed by writers
for Product Concept Mfg., Inc. or in a rare case,
the author is unknown.

Simple
Household
S lutions

Housework is something you do
that nobody notices until you don't do it.

~Author Unknown

Ever need a quick substitution for a recipe ingredient? Ever want housecleaning to go faster—and better? Ever wonder how to cut costs and trim expenses? Ever been stuck for an inexpensive and easy gift idea? If so, here's your go-to source for answers!

From cover to cover, you'll find practical hints for cooking, cleaning, doing laundry, storing stuff, and saving money. Plus, surprising uses for common household items, creative ideas for fun and functional gifts, and practical reuse-and-recycle tips. There are also tips for making celebrations and holidays fun and hassle-free. To top it all off, handy checklists to help you get organized and enjoy the peace of mind of knowing that you have the important stuff taken care of.

So why wait? Let's get on a roll!

TABLE OF CONTENTS

When mixing solutions, use caution and make sure to mix in a ventilated area.

CHAPTER 1
VERY CLEVER!
Before you dash to the store for a special product to take care of common household problems, scan these lists. There's a good chance you have what you need right in your own broom closet or kitchen cupboard!

CHAPTER 2
QUICK and EASY CLEAN-UP
Household tasks made quick and easy is what this section i all about. It's full of helpful hints on everything from tidying up to degreasing the kitchen, from de-clogging drains t removing laundry stains. Before you know it, you're done!

CHAPTER 3
IN THE KITCHEN

Who couldn't use a little help in the kitchen? Here are practical guides for measuring, cooking, roasting, and storing food. Need new ideas for entertaining, spicing up leftovers, or just doing something different? You've come to the right place!

CHAPTER 4
PRACTICAL AND PAINLESS MONEY-SAVING TIPS

Start saving money in little ways every day, and you'll find that you're actually saving quite a bit of cash each month. Another way to save? Repurpose what you already own instead for buying new, and adopt a few of our thrift living tips!

CHAPTER 5
CELEBRATIONS, HOLIDAYS, AND GIFTS MADE EASY!
No-stress festivities mean you can sit back, relax, and enjoy the occasion right along with your guests! They'll never know how easy it was to create the appetizer they're all raving about, or how inexpensive it was to decorate your home or give the perfect gift. And there's no need to tell them, either!

CHAPTER 6
IMPORTANT CHECKLISTS
Preparation protects you and your family against needless loss in the event of an emergency. The amount of time you spend filling out these four simple charts will be small, but will give you immeasurable peace of mind.

CHAPTER 1

Very Clever!

Why search for a grill brush when crumpled aluminum foil will do the job just as well? Why spend your money on one-purpose leather cleaner when a little egg white does the same thing? Why scrub to remove price-sticker goo when a dab of nail polish remover will take it right off?

You'll be amazed at how many common household problems you can solve with nothing more than a cup of vinegar…a few tablespoons of cornstarch…a handful of crunched-up eggshells.

Very clever!

Very Clever Uses for
ALUMINUM FOIL

- Sharpen scissors and garden shears by cutting several times into layers of folded foil.

- Use a crumpled wad of foil to clean and remove rust spots from your grill or firepit grate.

- Shape a cake by lining a cake pan with two layers of heavy-duty foil, and then folding foil to desired shape.

- Crinkle foil and use it to create texture as you work with paint or plaster.

- Remove sticky build-up on iron by running the iron over a piece of foil.

- Slide furniture across carpet by putting pieces of foil under the legs (dull side on the floor or carpet).

- Keep a roll of heavy duty foil in your car to use in a pinch, such as forming a funnel to add oil, or placing on ground to hold lug nuts when changing a tire.

Very Clever Uses for
ALUMINUM FOIL

- De-tarnish silver jewelry and other silver items by lining a pan with foil, filling it with hot water, and adding a couple teaspoons of salt or baking soda. Let items soak for a few minutes, rinse and dry.

- Insert a sheet of foil under a cloth napkin in serving baskets to keep bread and rolls warm longer.

- Deter insects from feasting on your garden veggies by adding strips of foil to the mulch you use around the plants.

- Wrap wet paint brushes and rollers in foil to keep them moist while you take breaks from your work.

- Quick cover-up to protect doorknobs and other trims from drips when you're painting: just cover with foil.

- Perfect cake-taker for potlucks and meal-taking occasions: wrap sturdy corrugated cardboard with foil, turn your baked cake onto foil to cool, decorate and take. No dishes need to be returned.

Very Clever Uses for
ALUMINUM FOIL

- Steam wrinkles out of garments by laying foil over ironing board, placing garment on the foil, and holding iron slightly above garment, releasing steam as you go.

- Deter birds from plate glass windows and sliding doors by hanging pieces of foil from strings attached to curtain rods or door frame.

- Keep your steel wool pot scrubber on a piece of foil to minimize rust.

- Best way to reheat pizza: Place it on a sheet of foil, fold foil over the crust to keep it from burning, and put it in a 350 degree oven for a couple of minutes, check often.

- Deter birds and deer from damaging trees and plants by hanging strips of foil from branches or poles.

- Insert wads of foil into shoes and boots before you store them to help keep their shape.

Very Clever Uses for
ALUMINUM FOIL

- Keep insects out of beverage glasses and cups by forming a foil lid; punch a straw through, or punch a small hole for sipping.

- Firm loose battery connections by folding a small piece of foil and fitting it snuggly between spring and battery.

- Go-to tool for all-things-school: foil-covered cardboard makes an artist's palette; protective book cover; shape-former and decoration for costumes and projects (form a hat or mask; cut out the shape of a lake for diorama).

Very Clever Uses for
COFFEE

- A few coffee beans in the bottom of a sugar bowl or salt shaker will keep the product flowing freely.

- Gardeners can clean dirty hands by scrubbing with a paste of coffee grounds and liquid hand soap.

Very Clever Uses for
COFFEE

- To keep fireplace ashes from flying around during clean-up, sprinkle them with damp coffee grounds first.

- Dried, used coffee grounds are said to repel ants. Dry grounds on a cookie sheet, then sprinkle them on anthills.

- Freeze leftover coffee in ice cube trays and use for undiluted, extra flavor in coffee smoothies or iced coffee.

- Used coffee grounds will help scrub a greasy pan clean.

- Mix carrot seeds with dry coffee before planting. It's a good fertilizer and helps the fine seeds stay in place. Great for radishes, too.

- A sachet of fresh ground coffee will absorb odors in your car. Fill a doubled section of old pantyhose with coffee to make an instant air freshener. Place under seat.

- Fishermen can keep their worm bait alive longer by mixing coffee grounds into the dirt before adding the worms.

Very Clever Uses for
COFFEE

- Acid-loving plants will bloom better with a mulch of used coffee grounds.

- Create your own sepia "watercolor" with regular brewed coffee.

- Place a bowl of ground coffee inside your fridge for a few days to absorb odors.

- Massage used coffee grounds into hands to get rid of strong smells like fish and garlic.

- Make a natural Easter dye by soaking eggs in very strong brewed coffee.

- Toast ground coffee for 30 minutes under a broiler, then use as a dry rub for steaks.

- Make scratches in wood disappear by rubbing with a paste of instant coffee and water.

- Make a body scrub by combining a tablespoon of ground coffee with a tablespoon of olive oil.

Very Clever Uses for
COFFEE

- Apply cool, strong coffee to clean, dry hair. Leave it on for 20 minutes, then rinse for extra-shiny hair.

- A touch of coffee in chocolate cake, brownies and desserts enhances the flavor.

- Get rid of old mothball smell in closed areas by putting a bowl of dry, used grounds sprinkled with a few drops of vanilla nearby.

- Dried used coffee grounds make a great homemade pin-cushion filler. Place in center of fabric square and tie tightly. Helps pins stay rust free and smells great.

Very Clever Uses for
CORNSTARCH

- Polish silver with a paste of cornstarch and water. Apply, dry and buff.

- Sprinkling cornstarch on a difficult knot will make it untangle more easily.

- Remove oil stains in your driveway by sprinkling liberally with cornstarch. Let sit overnight and rinse with hose.

- Make a dry shampoo by sprinkling hair with corn starch. Let sit a few minutes and brush out.

- Iron-scorched fabric can be fixed by wetting the burned area, covering it with cornstarch, and brushing it away after the starch has dried.

- Rub cornstarch on your rolling pin to prevent dough from sticking.

- For ink stains, treat the area with a paste of cornstarch and milk. Rub in, let dry, then brush off the residue.

Very Clever Uses for
CORNSTARCH

- Ease sunburn and insect bites by applying a paste of cornstarch and water. Let it dry on the skin, then rinse off.

- Creaky wood floors can be silenced by sweeping cornstarch into the seams where the boards rub together.

- Freshen mildewed books by applying cornstarch to pages. Allow to sit overnight, and shake off excess outdoors.

- Remove grease stains on your leather bag by applying cornstarch overnight. Brush away excess and stain should be gone.

- Keep playing cards from sticking together by shaking cards in a bag with a few tablespoons of cornstarch. Remove cards and wipe them off individually.

- Clean windows with a mixture of a gallon of water, a teaspoon of cornstarch and a teaspoon of dish soap. Spray on and wipe clean.

Very Clever Uses for
CORNSTARCH

- Make scented bath powder by mixing cornstarch with a few drops of essential oil. Use sparingly to prevent caking.

- Absorb smelly foot odors by sprinkling shoes with cornstarch.

- Make your own spray starch for ironing by dissolving a tablespoon of cornstarch in a pint of warm water. Put in a spray bottle.

- To remove bloodstains, rub area with paste of cornstarch and cold water. Let dry in the sun. Brush off and repeat if necessary.

- Freshen your dog's coat by sprinkling fur with cornstarch, then brushing out.

- Remove greasy stains on carpet by applying cornstarch to the stain. Let sit for a half hour, then vacuum.

- If your marshmallows are sticking together, sprinkle a little cornstarch into the bag and shake.

Very Clever Uses for
CORNSTARCH

- A bit of cornstarch applied to your hands will help prevent blistering when working in the garden.

- Freshen stuffed animals by applying a sprinkle of cornstarch. Let sit for 15 minutes, then vacuum them off.

- For easy homemade finger paints, mix a quarter cup of cornstarch with 2 cups of water. Boil to desired consistency, then divide into containers and add food coloring.

Very Clever Uses for
DRYER SHEETS

- Wipe furniture and kitchen counters with dryer sheets—dirt, dust, grit, and pet hair cling to the sheet.

- Tuck a sheet into toilet paper rolls for bathroom freshness.

- Clean latex paint from brushes by soaking them in a can of warm water along with a used dryer sheet.

Very Clever Uses for
DRYER SHEETS

- Place a dryer sheet on the bottom of the kitchen trash can to soak up any spills and help prevent bad odors.

- Keep a dryer sheet in the kitchen for dry-spill clean-ups; they're especially effective in wiping up flour spills.

- Keep a dryer sheet under the seat of your car for on-the-go fresh scents.

- Store threaded sewing needles in a sheet to prevent threads from tangling or slipping off; run threaded needles through a sheet to reduce knotting and tangling while you sew.

- Clean windows and blinds with used dryer sheets to easily remove dirt and dust.

- Drop a sheet in the dirty laundry hamper, diaper bag, gym bag, and suitcase to cut down on odors.

- Keep a dryer sheet in your purse as an instant static remover for hair and clothing. Bonus—your purse will remain smelling fresh and new!

Very Clever Uses for
DRYER SHEETS

- Moisten used dryer sheets to wipe washing machine and dryer, and clean the dryer's lint trap.

- Keep a dryer sheet in your dressing area; swipe it over clothing to remove powder or deodorant marks, lint, and pet hair. Bonus—that just-laundered scent!

- Wipe scissors with a used dryer sheet to remove minute particles that cause the blade to dull.

- Wipe lamp shades and curtains with used dryer sheets to capture dust and leave a fresh, clean smell.

- Remove crayon marks, gum, and candle wax from shelves and wood furniture by gently rubbing with a moistened dryer sheet.

- Eliminate the musty smell from old books or stored clothing by keeping them in a plastic bag along with a dryer sheet for a few days.

- Place dryer sheets in attics, basements, closets, and other storage areas to repel rodents and add a fresh smell.

Very Clever Uses for
DRYER SHEETS

- Give your office cubicle a fresh scent by placing a few dryer sheets in desk or file drawers.

- Wipe the dashboard of your car to pick up dust easily and leave behind a fresh, new-car scent.

- Soak tired feet in warm water and scrub with used dryer sheets for fresh scent and gentle softening action.

- Use a moistened dryer sheet to remove bug splats from the car windshield and grill.

- Tuck in a dryer sheet before storing tents, sleeping bags, and other camping gear to repel rodents and help eliminate musty odors.

Very Clever Uses for
EGGS AND EGGSHELLS

Good tip: When using eggshells, it's a good idea to bake them on a cookie sheet at 250 degrees for about 20 minutes to dry them out.

- Brush egg white onto the inside bottom of your baked piecrusts before filling to keep crust from getting soggy.

- Soak an eggshell in a cup of apple cider for a few days. Dab on minor skin irritations to soothe them.

- Clean hummingbird feeders by filling halfway with warm water. Add crushed eggshells, shake well, and rinse with hot water.

- Use egg white as a handy all-purpose glue for paper and cardboard.

- Brighten laundry by putting one or two clean broken eggshells and two lemon slices in a cheesecloth bag and tossing in your wash.

- Add nutrients to your outdoor plants by pouring cooled water from boiled eggs on them.

Very Clever Uses for
EGGS AND EGGSHELLS

- Use crushed eggshells around the bases of your garden plants to repel slugs and snails.

- Beat an egg with a tablespoon of olive oil until frothy, then apply to hair. Leave on for 20 minutes and rinse for a great natural conditioner.

- Mix ground eggshells with soapy water for an effective scrub for dirty pots and pans.

- Whisk egg whites with water and apply to a dry face for a pore-reducing facial. Allow to sit on skin for a few minutes and rinse off.

- Save eggshell halves and egg cartons. Filled with dirt and placed in the carton, they're a good way to start seedlings.

- Place crushed eggshells in the garden to help deter blossom end rot on tomato plants.

- Blow out and dry eggshells, and you have adorable gelatin molds for kids. Fill and peel off shell after gelatin is firm.

Very Clever Uses for
EGGS AND EGGSHELLS

- Clean tea stains out of a mug or pot by filling with crushed eggshells and letting it sit for a few hours. Add water and swish before pouring out the shells; rinse.

- Put eggshells in your garbage disposal to help clean the blades.

- Beat an egg white and apply a thin layer to dull or dirty leather. Rub in lightly to heighten shine.

- Add crushed eggshells around houseplants to deter cats from using the plants as litterboxes.

- Add crushed eggshells to ground coffee before brewing to make it less bitter.

- Combine one egg white and 1/4 cup water. Stir into your homemade stock to clarify it. Pour through a strainer to remove egg white.

- Remove gum on clothes by applying egg whites to gum with a toothbrush. Let sit for 15 minutes, and then launder as usual.

Very Clever Uses for
LEMONS

- Rub hands and cutting board with a lemon wedge after handling fish.

- Freeze lemon juice in an ice tray to use later in cooking.

- Put several lemons in a clear bowl or wire basket to create a sunny centerpiece.

- Squeeze lemon juice on hair before rinsing for shine and brightness.

- Rub hands, elbows, knees, and feet with a lemon wedge to remove roughness and discoloration.

- Burn a few lemon peels along with firewood to remove unpleasant fireplace odors.

- Simmer a sliced lemon to freshen the house. Add a few cinnamon sticks, if desired.

- Scrub cheese graters with a lemon wedge to remove stuck food particles.

Very Clever Uses for
LEMONS

- Brighten dull fingernails by scrubbing them with a lemon wedge.

- Remove tarnish on metals with a paste of lemon juice and baking soda.

- Add a halved lemon to the cavity of roast chicken for additional flavor and tenderness.

- Add lemon juice and honey to a cup of hot tea for relief from a sore throat.

- Wipe the inside of refrigerator, ice chest, and microwave with a sponge dipped in lemon juice to brighten and freshen surfaces.

- Repel bugs with lemon juice. Apply a few drops where ants enter; wipe counters and floors with lemon juice and water; make a sachet of dry lemon rinds for closets and drawers.

- Sprinkle lemon juice on cut fruit and guacamole to preserve color.

Very Clever Uses for
LEMONS

- Grind sliced lemon peels in garbage disposal to deodorize the drain.

- Remove laundry stains by soaking items in a mixture of lemon juice, baking soda, and water before washing. Sponge tough stains with lemon juice and let soak.

- Scrub plastic utensils with a lemon wedge to remove stubborn stains.

- Spritz the room with a spray bottle filled with lemon juice and water for a fresh, natural fragrance.

- Get whites white (including athletic shoes) by spraying them with lemon juice and drying them in the sun.

- Clean copper cookware with a lemon wedge sprinkled with salt.

- Secure a lemon wedge on a prong in your dishwasher for fresh-smelling, sparkling clean dishes.

- Keep rice from sticking by adding a teaspoon of lemon juice to the water.

Very Clever Uses for
LEMONS

- Make your own all-purpose cleaning solution by mixing lemon juice, white vinegar, and water.

- Make your own potpourri by drying lemon slices in a low oven, and then putting slices in sachets or decorative dishes.

Very Clever Uses for
NAIL POLISH AND REMOVER

Note: When using nail polish remover, test in hidden spot to make sure the product doesn't damage the surface.

- Dab clear nail polish to seal small holes in door and window screens.

- Coat mailing labels with clear nail polish to prevent ink from smudging.

- Use a neon-bright nail polish to mark numbers on your mail box.

Very Clever Uses for
NAIL POLISH AND REMOVER

- Add a dot of glow-in-the-dark nail polish to mark remote control button, keys, cell phones, and light switches.

- Paint over the rough edges of wooden and plastic hangers with nail polish to avoid snags in your clothing.

- Dab a bit of nail polish on ends of ribbon, rope, shoe laces, yarn, and twine to prevent fraying.

- Color-code keys and other objects with various brightly colored nail polishes.

- Thread needles easily by dipping the tip of the thread in nail polish; let dry before threading.

- Keep costume jewelry from tarnishing by coating it with clear nail polish; add to the backs of inexpensive bracelets, necklaces, and watches to help eliminate an allergic reaction to the metals.

- Coat the threads of screws with nail polish before setting them so they will hold tightly.

Very Clever Uses for
NAIL POLISH AND REMOVER

- Apply a dab of bright nail polish on the bottoms of dishes and containers you take to potluck events for easy ID at the end of the meal.

- Fix small nicks on decorative glassware and fashion shoes with a dab of nail polish that closely matches the original color.

- Create cool accessories by using glitzy, glittery nail polish to paint fun patterns on bobby pins, decorative combs, barrettes, plastic headbands, sunglasses, and small plastic purses.

- Control damage to fabric by dabbing the edges of frayed seams and small tears with clear nail polish.

- Try nail polish if you're out of glue to repair jewelry or for other small patch-ups.

- Get rid of sticker goo with acetone-based polish remover.

- Remove ink, permanent marker, and super glue by rubbing with acetone-based polish remover.

Very Clever Uses for
NAIL POLISH AND REMOVER

- Wipe vases and decorative glassware with a cotton ball soaked in acetone-based polish remover to eliminate stubborn stains.

- Remove paint splatters from windows, mirrors, and glass doors by blotting with acetone-based polish remover; let soak for a few minutes and then wipe clean.

- Clear scratches from a watch face by gently rubbing glass with acetone-based polish remover.

- Clean scuff marks from tiles floors with acetone-based polish remover.

Very Clever Uses for
COOKING OIL

- Polish leather shoes with olive oil. Apply liberally with a soft cloth, then buff with a soft rag.

- Swallow a tablespoon of olive oil to soothe a scratchy throat.

- Use a cotton ball to apply oil to squeaky hinges.

- Massage a small amount of oil onto your face for a wonderful moisturizer.

- Protect garden tools by coating them with oil before storing them. It will keep them cleaner and deter rust.

- Rub a tad of oil onto the inside of your candle holders before inserting tapers and drips will peel right off.

- Coat the inside of measuring cups with oil to help sticky liquids like corn syrup, molasses and honey slide right out.

- Scrub sticky hands with a paste of oil and coarse salt. Rinse well.

Very Clever Uses for
COOKING OIL

- Add a few drops of olive oil to your cat's food to help prevent hairballs.

- Add a teaspoon of oil to your dog's food to help maintain a glossy coat.

- Shine stainless steel by rubbing it with oil and a soft rag.

- Condition dry cuticles by massaging them with warm oil.

- Season a cast-iron skillet by rubbing the inside with oil, then place into a 350° oven for 30 minutes.

- Condition your scalp by massaging it with warm olive oil. Leave it on for 30 minutes before shampooing.

- Peel off stickers the easy way by applying oil and then letting it soak in.

- Soothe chapped lips with a thin coat of oil.

Very Clever Uses for
COOKING OIL

- Prevent cracking of wicker and rattan by rubbing it with warm oil. Apply with paintbrush to crevices then wipe off with a soft cloth.

- Use a dab of oil on a cotton swab to help free a stuck zipper. Avoid contact with fabric.

- Add a few tablespoons of olive oil to your bath water to help soften skin.

- Rub olive oil on dry, cracked elbows and heels daily to soften.

Very Clever Uses for
RICE

- Clean narrow-neck vases by filling 2/3 full with warm water. Add a tablespoon or two of uncooked rice. Cover the opening and shake container for several minutes. Dump out rice and rinse.

- Clean electric coffee grinders by filling them with uncooked white rice. Run the grinder, and the oils will adhere to the rice. Dump out residue.

- Put 1/2 teaspoon of uncooked white rice in your salt shaker to keep it flowing freely.

- Place uncooked rice inside a spare sock and knot for a microwaveable heat pack.

- Dry off a wet cell phone by immersing it in a bowl of dry rice overnight. (Disconnect the battery first.)

- Use uncooked rice as a pie weight when baking an unfilled pie crust. Place a cup of rice on tin foil then place foil on crust.

- Store fruit in a container with rice to speed up the ripening. Check frequently to avoid over-ripening.

Very Clever Uses for
RICE

- Get the dust off of silk flowers by shaking them for a minute in a closed bag along with a cup of rice. Shake any rice off after removing from bag.

- Drop a grain of rice into the oil when deep-frying food. If it rises to the surface and begins cooking, the oil is ready. Carefully remove rice with slotted spoon.

- Save excess water from cooked rice. Cooled, use it to wash your face. Rinse well for a radiant glow.

- Place an open container of uncooked rice in toolbox to help keep tools from rusting.

- Add a half cup of uncooked rice to your blender and run it for a few minutes to sharpen blades.

- Add color to uncooked rice and use in clear vases for silk flowers or votive holders. To color, put a cup of rice in a plastic bag, add a few drops of rubbing alcohol and food coloring, and shake well. Allow to dry.

- Dry out wet boots overnight by filling soles with an inch of dry rice. Pour out in the morning.

Very Clever Uses for
RICE

- Fill a kitchen crock with several inches of uncooked rice and insert kitchen knives, blade down, for an accessible holder.

- Remove coffee stains from the bottom of coffee pots and carafes by pouring in a few tablespoons of rice and a half cup of ice cubes. Swirl around and rinse.

- Use a rice paste to fix over-salted soup or stew. Puree 1/2 cup of unsalted cooked white rice with water to make a thin paste. Stir into your soup.

Very Clever Uses for
SALT

- Pour a mixture of salt and hot water down kitchen sink to prevent grease from collecting in drain.

- Pour salt into patio crevices and in between bricks, then sprinkle with hot water, to prevent weeds.

- Add salt to bee stings to relieve ache and reduce swelling.

- Sprinkle frying pan with salt to minimize grease splatters when frying.

- Rub dry, flaky skin with salt for an inexpensive, natural exfoliator.

- Gargle with salt water to freshen breath or soothe a sore throat.

- Remove dish marks or beverage rings from wood with a paste of salt and salad oil.

- Clean bottom of steam iron by sprinkling salt on news paper or wax paper. Run hot iron over the surface.

- Add a pinch of salt to pasta water for a higher boiling temperature and quicker cooking.

- Sprinkle a little salt into athletic shoes to help remove moisture and odor.

- Add a handful of salt to fireplace flames for a colorful glow and to help loosen soot and residue for easier clean-up.

- Apply a paste of salt and water to baked- or burned-on foods on cookware. Let soak, and then wash.

- Enhance the flavor of coffee by adding a dash of salt in coffee water before brewing.

- Reduce puffiness around the eyes with a paste of salt and warm water. Gently apply to eye area with a cotton ball.

- Loosen greasy food stains on carpet with a solution of salt and rubbing alcohol.

- Sprinkle a little salt over salads to keep greens crisp.

Very Clever Uses for
SALT

- Add a pinch of salt to a vase of cut flowers to preserve freshness.

- Remove deposits left by flowers in vase by filling vase with salted water.

- Relieve itchiness from poison ivy rash by soaking affected area in warm saltwater.

- Free bathroom sink drains of hair and soap residue with a mixture of salt, baking soda, and white vinegar. Pour down drain, lct soak, and then flush with boiling water.

- Remove lipstick stains from glasses by rubbing the rims with salt before washing.

- Deodorize travel mugs, thermoses, and decanters by filling with salt and warm water. Rinse thoroughly.

- Remove dust from silk flowers by putting them in a bag along with 1/4 cup of salt; shake gently.

Very Clever Uses for
SHAMPOO & DISH SOAP

- Soak fingernails in dish soap to soften cuticles and remove oils from nails so new polish will adhere well. Rinse well and dry before adding new polish.

- Clean blenders and food processors by pouring in a dab of dish soap and a cup of water; run unit for a few minutes, and then empty, rinse well, and dry.

- Combine a small amount of dish soap, a cup of salt, and a gallon of white vinegar for an effective weed killer. Pour in patio and driveway crevices where weeds sprout.

- Spray a solution of dish soap and water on areas where ants enter the house to discourage further invasion.

- Soak greasy yard and automotive tools in a mixture of dish soap and water to remove oils.

- Clean and shine solid-surface floor with a solution of water and dish soap.

- Soak metal mesh A/C air filters in dish soap and warm water; rinse clean; dry.

Very Clever Uses for
SHAMPOO & DISH SOAP

- De-grease kitchen cabinets, counters, and appliances by wiping them with dish soap diluted in water; wipe again with clean water; dry to prevent streaking.

- Clean and de-grease door handles with dish soap and water.

- Mix dish soap or shampoo and water with a drop of glycerin in a jar for kid's bubble-blowing solution; form a wand out of wire.

- Get stains out of clothing by soaking the spot in dish soap or shampoo before laundering.

- Buff leather shoes and purses with a dab of shampoo for shine and freshness.

- Clean paint brushes by soaking them in lukewarm water with a dab of shampoo added.

- Dab shampoo around the edges of an adhesive bandage for easy and ouch-free removal.

Very Clever Uses for
SHAMPOO & DISH SOAP

- Get a zipper to glide easily by dabbing a small amount of shampoo on the teeth of the zipper.

- Remove make-up, including mascara, with baby shampoo and a damp cloth; rinse face thoroughly with warm water.

- Loosen tight screws by dabbing shampoo around the head and letting the shampoo soak into the threads.

- Hand wash delicate fabrics in a small amount of shampoo in warm water; rinse.

- Soak combs and brushes in warm water and a dab of shampoo; rinse; dry thoroughly.

- Apply a few drops of shampoo to quiet squeaky hinges.

- Remove dust from the leaves of houseplants by wiping with a few drops of shampoo and water.

Very Clever Uses for
VINEGAR

Note: When applying vinegar to fabric, upholstery, wood, or other surfaces, test a hidden area to make sure no staining or damage occurs.

- Boost dishwasher cleaning power by pouring two cups of white vinegar in the bottom of dishwasher; add soap; wash full cycle.

- Wipe windows with a mixture of half white vinegar and half warm water to avoid streaks.

- Clean microwave by bringing one cup water and 1/4 cup white vinegar to a boil; then wipe down microwave.

- Sanitize doorknobs, handles, and safety bars by wiping with a sponge soaked in white vinegar.

- Remove corrosion from faucets and showerheads by saturating a towel with vinegar and wrapping it around corroded area; let soak, then wipe clean.

- Keep clothes and blankets fresh by adding a cup of white vinegar to laundry during rinse cycle.

Very Clever Uses for
VINEGAR

- Scrub birdbaths with white vinegar; rinse thoroughly.

- Remove fruit and berry stains from your hands by rubbing them with vinegar.

- Remove deodorant and some cosmetic stains from clothing by rubbing with white vinegar, and then washing as usual.

- Loosen chewing gum or sticky candy from carpets and upholstery by dabbing area with white vinegar.

- Remove sticky goo left by labels, stickers, decals, and bumper stickers by wiping repeatedly with white vinegar.

- Soak gold jewelry in apple cider vinegar for 15 minutes. Remove and dry.

- Soak vintage lace and fabric in white vinegar and warm water to freshen and reduce stains; wash with mild detergent.

Very Clever Uses for
VINEGAR

- Wipe down outdoor tables and chairs with a sponge soaked in white vinegar to freshen and sanitize.

- Add a teaspoon of vinegar to water when boiling white potatoes to keep them white.

- Rub seasoned vinegar and oil on steaks for increased flavor and tenderness; let stand for several hours before cooking.

- Eliminate unpleasant cooking odors by simmering a mixture of vinegar and water.

- Relieve dry skin by adding a few tablespoons of vinegar to bathwater.

- Eliminate doggy odor and add shine to a canine coat by adding a cup of white vinegar to the pet's rinse water when bathing.

- Reduce frost and ice build-up on auto windshield by wiping with a solution of three parts white vinegar and one part water.

Very Clever Uses for
VINEGAR

- Remove deposits and discoloration from flower pots and planters by soaking them in white vinegar for several hours.

Very Clever Solutions to
PESKY PROBLEMS

- Place bay leaves, cloves, or sage at their point of entrance to keep ants out of the house.

- Plant a garlic bulb in the container to keep bugs out of potted plants.

- Place a kitty-sized box or basket on your desk or work table to give kitty an alternative spot to nap. Enhance the spot with catnip, if needed. Kitty will curl up happily in her new space, and you can get back to work!

Very Clever Solutions to
PESKY PROBLEMS

- Keep computer and TV vents dust- and pet-hair free by wiping frequently with a microfiber cloth.

- Clean computer keyboard and remote control with a damp cloth; use a small paint brush to remove dust and other particles from between the keys.

- Clean computer and TV screens by lightly wiping the screen with a microfiber cloth or soft, lint-free cotton cloth. Use broad strokes across the surface of the screen. If smudges or fingerprints remain, power down the device; gently wipe screen with a damp cloth. Allow surface to air dry before restoring power.

- Cover open recipe books with a piece of clear acrylic glass (available at hardware and home improvement stores) while you cook. If the glass gets smudged or splattered, you can put it in the dishwasher.

- Make your own fireplace kindling! Fill empty toilet paper rolls with tightly wadded newspaper or shredded paper.

- Water ferns with weak tea to give them a boost.

Very Clever Solutions to
PESKY PROBLEMS

- Keep recipe printouts in acrylic sleeves to keep pages clean.

- Add two tablespoons of white vinegar and two tea spoons of sugar to the water to maintain the freshness of cut flowers.

- Indoor plants – Save water from boiling eggs or pasta. When cooled, pour on plants to give extra nutrients.

- Periodically wipe leaves of broad-leafed indoor plants with a damp cloth to remove dust.

- Soak diamond rings in soapy water and brush gently with an old toothbrush to restore sparkle.

- Touch up minor scratches on wood furniture with matching or near-matching markers.

- Use square plastic bread tabs to mark your place on a roll of tape.

- Rub your hands on a stainless steel sink faucet or spoon to remove garlic odor.

Very Clever Solutions to
PESKY PROBLEMS

- Create a tasty meal or snack for a small child who tolerates no one food touching another by filling sections in an ice cube tray with child-pleasing delicacies, such as, bits of meat and veggies; mini-chunks of cheese; broken crackers or cookies; a dollop of applesauce, mashed potatoes, pudding.

- Stretch a thick rubber band around the paint can (top to bottom). Use it to remove excess paint from your brush as you work.

- Rub minor scratches on glass surfaces with a dab of white toothpaste; repeat; wipe off excess toothpaste.

- Rub petroleum jelly on spigot and garden hose nozzle so the hose can be easily removed.

CHAPTER 2

Quick and Easy Clean-Up

Hate housework? You'll find it is not-so-bad (and maybe even fun) when you get cleaning day simplified and organized. In this section, you'll find dozens of useful tips and easy tricks to help you get the job done efficiently so you don't waste time on do-overs. You'll learn what professionals do to leave kitchens and bathrooms sparkling, and bedrooms and living areas clean, neat, and dust-free. In addition, our Brilliant Solutions will help you take care of even the toughest housecleaning and laundry challenges!

You won't hate housework when you love how your home-sweet-home looks when it's done!

SIX GOOD, CLEAN HABITS

KEEP THE APPOINTMENT
Set aside time each week for housecleaning. A concentrated effort for even a short amount of time will yield visible results.

MUSTER THE TROOPS
Get the whole family involved. Even small children can take on simple tasks, like picking up toys or bringing sheets and towels to the laundry room. Remember, many hands make light work!

STASH THE SMALL STUFF
Clean-up is easier and goes faster when you de-clutter first. If the project seems daunting at first, break it down into small achievable tasks. Maybe even put on some lively music that keeps you moving! Take 15 or 20 minutes a day to clean out one closet, a set of shelves or cabinets, or room. Any items you no longer need or want can be thrown out, recycled, donated to charity, or put aside for a garage sale. The time will pass—and you'll have a completely de-cluttered home—before you know it!

SIX GOOD, CLEAN HABITS

COME CLEAN

Adopt a clean-as-you-go philosophy to avoid facing a series of monumental tasks at the end of the week. Wipe spills when they happen; put products back in the cupboard after you've used them; file paper, documents, and mail where it belongs instead of throwing it in a pile for "later."

SPECIAL TASKS

Each cleaning day, fit in one small housecleaning chore that doesn't need doing every time.

INVEST IN CLEAN!

Buy good cleaning tools for your home. The right vacuum, sweepers, brooms, mops, and dusters will do the job efficiently and effectively, and leave you feeling proud of your work. Keep cleaning products and supplies in one place so you can easily reach for the ones you need.

Completely Clean
KITCHEN

- Remove stains from non-stick pans by boiling 2 Tbs. baking soda, 1/2 cup vinegar, and 1 cup water until stains disappear.

- Clean and shine the bottoms of copper pans by setting pans in a dish of pickle juice for 15 minutes. Rinse and dry.

- Freshen and sanitize trash container by filling with 1 cup bleach along with water; allow to soak, then rinse.

- Polish stainless steel by sprinkling baking soda on a damp sponge and wiping to a nice shine.

- Use toothpaste to remove tarnish from silver utensils and other items. Apply, rub, and then wipe with a clean sponge.

- Brew a solution of white vinegar and water through coffeemaker to clean and freshen; brew again with plain water to rinse.

- Degrease cabinets and kitchen appliances with a solution of white vinegar and water; wipe with a damp sponge, then wipe again with plain water.

- Freshen blenders and food processors by filling bowl with a 50/50 solution of baking soda and water; run for several minutes; rinse and dry.

- Rub tomato paste or ketchup on copper and brass items to clean; rinse and shine.

- Boil apple peels in an aluminum pan to restore its color and luster.

- Sprinkle salt into milk-scorched pans, let sit, then scrub and rinse. For non-stick pans, rinse salt away before scrubbing.

- Sprinkle a layer of baking soda on cutting boards to deodorize; sprinkle with water, then allow to sit overnight before rinsing.

Completely Clean
KITCHEN

- Clean and shine floors by mopping with a solution of white vinegar and water; dry immediately.

- Get rid of tomato stains in plastic containers and on plastic stirring spoons by washing them in cold—not hot—water.

- Wash your hand operated can opener in hot, sudsy water after each use to avoid cross-contamination.

- Reduce odor when cooking fish by first soaking fish in a solution of water and vinegar. For additional odor control, boil a pan of water and vinegar while cooking fish.

- Freshen sponges and pot scrubbers by putting them in the dishwasher flatware try.

- Remove garlic and onion smells on cutting boards by sprinkling salt on the surface and rubbing down with a lemon wedge.

Completely Clean
KITCHEN

- Disinfect kitchen sponges and dishrags by soaking them in a solution of one quart water and 1/4 cup bleach. Rinse and dry.

- Wipe down plastic cutting boards with bleach to prevent mold. Rinse thoroughly.

- Get the whole family in the habit of taking dishes directly to the dishwasher rather than stacking them on the counter or leaving them in the sink.

- Keep the kitchen smelling fresh by baking orange peels at 350 for a couple of minutes.

BUCK THE MUCK, QUELL THE SMELL, REFINE THE SHINE!

BLENDER, FOOD PROCESSOR
Unplug unit. All removable parts can be washed in dish soap. Do not soak blades, but dip in soapy water, rinse, and dry. Wipe down base with a damp sponge and a solution of white vinegar and water, being careful not to get motor area wet. Dry all parts completely before reassembling. To freshen inside, add 1 part baking soda to 1 part water in bowl and mix for a few minutes; rinse and dry bowl.

BRASS HANDLES
Put brass cabinet handles in a saucepan and cover with catsup. Bring to a boil, then turn down the heat and let soak until handles look shiny. Rinse and buff dry.

CLOGGED DRAIN
Pour about 1 cup baking soda and 1 cup white vinegar down the drain. After an hour, flush with boiling water. Or, put several denture cleaner down the drain, then flush with boiling water. If grease is causing the clog, pour 1 cup salt water and 1 cup baking soda down the drain; after an hour, flush with boiling water.

CABINETS
Exterior – Degrease with a solution of white vinegar and water; or baking soda and water. Loosen tough grease with a paste of baking soda and a few drops of water. Rinse thoroughly to avoid streaking. Interior – Vacuum out loose food particles, and remove hardened food by scraping with a plastic knife or food scraper. For easy maintenance, line shelves with shelf paper; keep drip-prone containers on a tray. Place an open box of baking soda inside cupboards to remove odors; if odor persists, wipe down interior with a solution of white vinegar and water; or place a bowl of white vinegar inside the cabinet and allow to sit for a week.

COFFEE MAKER
To remove coffee residue, perk or run a solution of white vinegar and water through the unit; follow with a cycle of plain water. Wash removable parts in dish soap and hot water.

COOKWARE
Remove burned food by covering bottom of pan with dish soap and a little water; let stand overnight, and wash clean. Or, place a dryer sheet in the pan along with hot water; let stand overnight, and wash clean. For quick results, add about an inch of water along with dish soap, and bring the solution to a boil; allow to cool, then wash.

To clean burned milk, sprinkle the bottom of the pan with salt and let sit for about 10 minutes before scrubbing. (Rinse salt from a nonstick pan before scrubbing, as salt can scratch the surface.)

ALUMINUM – Never put aluminum cookware in the dishwasher. Remove inside discoloration by filling pan with a solution of 1 tablespoon cream of tartar or lemon juice to each quart of water. Simmer until discoloration has disappeared (usually about 10 minutes). Scrub outside of pan with a soapy steel-wool sponge.

COPPER – Scrub with a slice of lemon sprinkled with salt. Or, scrub with a paste of 1 tablespoon each of salt, white vinegar, and flour. Or, coat with a layer of catsup, and let sit for 30 minutes. Wash in warm soapy water, rinse, and dry.

ENAMEL – Cool before washing to avoid cracking the enamel surface. Gently rub with a synthetic scouring pad to remove burned-on food. Or, fill pan with warm water and add 1-3 denture cleaners. Rinse and wipe when the fizzies fade.

NONSTICK SURFACES – Mix 2 tablespoons baking soda with 1 cup of water and 1/2 cup vinegar. Boil the mixture in the pan until stains disappear. Rub stubborn stains with a cloth or sponge dipped in white vinegar. Wash and rinse.

STAINLESS STEEL – Cover stain for 30 minutes in 2 cups white vinegar; wash and rinse. Or, sprinkle stain with baking soda, cover with water, and bring to a boil; wash and rinse. Keep stainless steel cookware and utensils shiny by sprinkling baking soda on the surface and polish with a damp sponge; or apply waterless hand soap and wipe off.

COUNTERTOPS
For most surfaces, wipe with a solution of white vinegar and water. For stubborn stains, apply a paste of baking soda and a few drops of water and let soak for a few minutes. Rub gently before rinsing. Follow manufacturer instructions for special surfaces.

GRANITE – Sprinkle with baking soda and wipe with a damp cloth or sponge. Apply a paste of baking soda and a few drops of water on stubborn stains; cover with a damp paper towel and allow to sit overnight. Wet down, rub gently, and rinse.

MARBLE – To polish surface, dip a damp cloth into finely crushed white chalk (regular chalkboard chalk). Wipe marble with overlapping strokes and let dry; rinse well; dry with soft clean cloth.

CUTTING BOARDS

Remove odor by sprinkling baking powder on board and scrubbing with a damp sponge. If odor persists, apply a paste of baking soda and a few drops of water and allow to sit overnight before rinsing.

DINNERWARE

To remove spots and film on glassware and utensils, soak items in a solution of white vinegar and water. To remove black or gray marks on plates, scrub with a mild, abrasive cleanser.

DISHWASHER

Wipe exterior with a solution of white vinegar and water. To remove yellow stains from interior, add a package of instant orange beverage crystals to a wash cycle, and allow dishwater to complete with rinse. To freshen interior, add several lemon slices to the utensil container before running dishes through a normal cycle.

FLOORS

LINOLEUM – Wipe with a damp mop; use a small amount of mild detergent in water if needed. To restore natural oils, add a few drops of baby oil to rinse water. Dry completely, as moisture can loosen seams.

STONE – Use a special cleaner for stone, or mop with a small amount of mild detergent and water.

TILE – Wipe with damp mop. To clean grout, mop with a solution of 1 capful rubbing alcohol to 1 gallon water; scrub stubborn stains with a old toothbrush.

VINYL – Mop with a solution of vinegar and water.

WOOD – Remove all loose dirt with broom or vacuum. Mop with a solution of vinegar and water; dry immediately, as standing water can warp surface.

GARBAGE DISPOSAL
To degrease the drain and remove food particles, pour baking soda into the drain and follow with white vinegar until foaming starts. After 10 minutes, flush with hot water. To freshen the drain, grind a few thinly cut lemon, lime, or orange slices. To sharpen blades, grind several ice cubes.

MICROWAVE
EXTERIOR – With a soft cloth or sponge, wipe with a solution of baking soda and water; or a solution of vinegar and water.

INTERIOR – Add 2 tablespoons lemon juice to 1 cup water and heat on High for about 5 minutes to loosen food particles; wipe down with a damp sponge. If stains remain, add 1 cup white vinegar to 1 cup water; heat on High for about 5 minutes; wipe down with a damp sponge. Remove the turntable and wash with dish soap and hot water. Dry thoroughly before reinserting the plate.

ODORS– Add lemon, lime, or orange slices, or a few drops of vanilla extract, to a bowl of water and heat on High for 30 seconds.

OVEN
Wipe with mild dish soap and water; rinse thoroughly. Glass window – wipe with dish soap and hot water; rinse. Apply a nonabrasive cleaner to tough stains. To freshen inside, heat an oven-safe bowl of water and vinegar at 350 degrees for 30 minutes.

PLASTIC CONTAINERS AND UTENSILS
To remove food stains from plastic, soak in a solution of 1 part bleach to 2 parts water; or, add denture cleaner tablets to water and let soak; wash and rinse thoroughly. Some red sauce stains on plastic are permanent.

RANGE

Remove drip pans and wash in warm soapy water. For stubborn stains, apply a paste of baking soda and a few drops of water, let sit for 30 minutes before scrubbing clean. Some burners can be removed and gently scrubbed, although never submerged in water. Wipe surface in a solution of white vinegar and water.

RANGE HOOD

Remove metal filters or screens and wash in dishwasher, or with hot soapy water. To remove thick grease, spray with oven cleaner before washing.

REFRIGERATOR/FREEZER

INTERIOR – Remove all food. Wipe down with a solution of baking soda and water. Removable trays can be washed with dish soap. Keep odor-free by placing an open box of baking soda inside both refrigerator and freezer.

EXTERIOR – Wipe down with a solution of white vinegar and water; rinse and dry thoroughly to avoid streaks.

SINK

PORCELAIN – Place paper towels on the bottom and soak with bleach; let stand before rinsing thoroughly.

STAINLESS STEEL – To remove water spots, wipe sink with a cloth dipped in rubbing alcohol.

TRASH CONTAINER

To disinfect and deodorize, pour 1 cup bleach and fill with water; allow to soak before rinsing. Use plastic liners for freshness.

WINDOWS

Wipe panes with a solution of white vinegar and water; dry with a wad of newspaper (use gloves to avoid getting print on your hands). Wipe frames and sills with a solution of white vinegar and water. Remove and vacuum screens, or rinse in hot water in sink.

Completely Clean
BATHROOM

- Get rid of mold on bathroom tiles by spraying area with a 50/50 mixture of bleach and water. Let sit, then rinse thoroughly.

- Hang a plastic grocery bag on the door handle for easy disposal of cleaning rags.

- Go a little greener by using cheap wash clothes purhased at a dollar store. Wash and reuse.

Completely Clean
BATHROOM

- Apply a paste of baking soda and water around sink drains to remove discoloration and soap scum.

- When you are finished cleaning the toilet bowl add a couple of drops of your favorite essential oil; peppermint or citrus. This will coat the bowl for easier cleaning and leave a clean fresh scent.

- Use baby wipes on delicate surfaces. They will leave them sparkly clean.

- On your silver faucets and fixtures use toothpaste to keep them bright and clean.

- Keep the mirrors from fogging by rubbing a small amount of liquid soap onto the suface. Buff for a fog-free finish.

Completely Clean
BEDROOMS AND LIVING AREAS

- Use a microfiber duster on tables, shelves, and solid-surface furniture. One swipe will do it!

- Vacuum carpet from one end of the room to the other, going over each area slowly, but only once. You'll save time and effort!

- Vacuum lampshades, drapery, and upholstery using a low suction setting on your vacuum along with a dusting-brush attachment.

- Use a lint roller to remove dust from solid-surface lampshades.

- Freshen rooms with a potpourri of flower petals or a dish of lemon slices.

Brilliant Solutions!
CARPET, FLOOR, FURNITURE
and More for Spot Clean-up

For all household stains, the best tip is to tend to them as soon as possible before they have time to set. For carpet and upholstery always test the stain removal hint on an inconspicuous area before attacking the stain.

CARPETS

- Blot, don't scrub the stain with a clean rag, working from the outside in. Rinse with clean water, and then repeat the process. Always blot after treating, with an absorbent, clean towel to remove excess moisture. Do not over-saturate through to the backing.

- Quick Mix: For most stains, use a solution of 1/2 teaspoon of non-bleaching laundry detergent mixed with 32 oz. of water.

- To remove wax or oil, place a paper towel over the stain and press with a warm iron. Repeat with clean towel until the wax is absorbed, then rinse with the Quick Mix.

- To remove gum, place an ice cube over the gum to freeze it hard, then use a dull knife to shatter it. Vacuum up hard pieces before they become sticky, and then blot area with a damp towel.

- For urine, absorb as much as possible with towels, then dab with a damp cloth. Blot with a solution of 1 part white vinegar to 1 part water. Dab again with a clean towel. Next use the detergent/water solution (Quick Mix), blot, rinse, and blot dry.

- Juice, coffee and tea stains can be treated by pouring club soda over the stain, then blotting and repeating the process. Use detergent/water solution (Quick Mix) to finish the process.

- For thick stains, like mud or oatmeal, allow to dry and vacuum and brush away residue. Then treat with detergent/water solution (Quick Mix).

UPHOLSTERY

- Avoid spraying water directly on upholstery because it can leave a ring. To remove stains, scrape off excess material with a spoon. Then, using a damp towel, work over the stain in a circular motion from the outside in. Rinse cloth and repeat until stain is removed.

- Baby wipes work well on carpet and upholstery stains. They contain gentle cleaners and evaporate quickly.

- Clean leather furniture with saddle soap.

WOOD FURNITURE

- To remove water rings on wood furniture, apply a generous amount of mayonnaise or cooking oil to the ring and let sit several hours. Wipe off with a soft dry cloth. An alternative method is to mix baking soda and non-gel toothpaste, and use a slightly damp cloth to rub the stain away.

- For nicks on wood furniture, take a raw pecan, almond, or walnut, break it in half and rub the nut edge into the nick. Experiment to see which nut works best with your wood. Wipe off excess with a dry cloth.

BATHROOM STAINS

- To remove rust stains on porcelain, use a pumice stick. Gently scrub the wet surface to avoid scratching. Once clean, rinse and wipe dry.

- For hard water stains, sprinkle wet surface with borax, let sit for a few minutes, rinse and dry.

- To clean stains in the toilet, pour 3 cups of vinegar into the bowl and scrub.

- Remove hairspray residue on bathroom mirrors by wiping with rubbing alcohol.

BEDROOM

- To freshen your mattress remove all bedding. Sprinkle a half box of plain baking soda directly onto the mattress. Vacuum thoroughly after a few hours.

- To remove dampness in a closet, try simple classroom chalk. A bowl of chalk on your closet shelf will help absorb excess humidity.

- When washing pillows, add vinegar to the final rinse. To dry, throw a clean pair of sneakers in the dryer to keep the pillows fluffed and to shorten drying time.

Brilliant Solutions!
PATIO, PORCH and MORE
Cleaning and Care for Outdoors

- Remove dust and grime from outdoor furniture by wiping it down with a solution of a cup of baking soda and 2 cups of warm water. Rinse thoroughly.

- Freshen the carpet in your car by sprinkling it with baking soda. Let sit for one hour and vacuum well.

- For stains on your car's leather or vinyl upholstery, rub a dab of toothpaste into the stain and remove excess. Test on an inconspicuous area first.

- To clean your exterior windshields, use a solution of 1/2 cup baking soda and a quart of warm water. Use a nylon bath pouf as a scrubber, apply and rinse well.

- Clean screens by dipping a damp brush in baking soda and scrubbing them. Rinse with a damp sponge or towel, or use a hose if screens have been removed.

- Charcoal briquettes absorb moisture and will help prevent rust in your tool box and metal garage cabinets.

- Remove rust on metal furniture with equal parts salt and cream of tartar, moistened with enough water to make a paste. Apply with a soft cloth and place item in sun to dry. Wipe off and repeat if necessary. Rinse clean.

- Streak-free window cleaner: 1/2 cup sudsy ammonia, 1 pint rubbing alcohol, 1 teaspoon of dishwashing liquid and one gallon of water.

- Clean outdoor cushions: mix 1 teaspoon dishwashing detergent, 1 quart warm water, and 1 tablespoon borax. Put in spray bottle and spray both sides to saturate and penetrate creases. Let sit for 15 minutes, rinse with hose. Dry, standing on edge in direct sun.

- Get white plastic furniture gleaming by mixing 3 tablespoons of automatic dishwasher detergent in a gallon of hot water. Apply with sponge, let sit 15 minutes and rinse. Because dishwasher detergent contains bleach, use on white furniture only.

- To remove oil stains on concrete, first blot with news paper. Then cover with cat litter for 8-10 hours. Sweep up litter, and repeat process till all oil is absorbed.

- Clear weeds growing in sidewalk cracks by pouring boiling water on them. Be careful not to splash yourself.

- Clean vinyl siding by mixing a cup of all-purpose cleaner in a bucket of warm water. Apply with a long handled, soft bristled brush scrubbing lengthwise. Rinse with hose after finishing each section.

- Garden tools can be cleaned by inserting them into a mixture of 5 gallons of sand and 3/4 cup mineral oil. Push tool blades into damp sand to clean and store them.

- To prevent garden diseases from spreading, always disinfect tools with a bleach solution between uses.

- Remove mold and fungus from flowerpots by scrubbing with a brush and a solution of 1 part chlorine bleach to 10 parts water. Rinse well, and dry thoroughly before using.

Brilliant Solutions!
SPOT AND STAIN REMOVAL
for Laundry

Test ANY stain removal method on an inconspicuous place before treating whole stain.

- Greasy stains: Rub detergent into stained area before washing.

- Non-greasy stains: Soak stain in cold water for at least 30 minutes.

- Remove stains completely before drying or ironing to avoid them becoming permanently heat-set.

- Blood stains: Flush with cold water as soon as possible, then soak in warm water and detergent. If yellow spot remains, dab with a cloth soaked in laundry bleach.

- Ketchup and Tomato sauce stains: Flush with cold water, then treat with laundry detergent and rinse. Blot the spot with white vinegar before washing.

- Chocolate: Rinse in warm water, apply stain remover to spot and add laundry bleach to the wash, if safe for the fabric.

- Coffee and tea: Soak stain in very hot water before washing.

- Cosmetics: Mix equal parts white vinegar and dishwashing liquid and rub into stained area before washing.

- Fruit punch: Treat with laundry detergent, and rinse. If stain remains, soak the item in a solution of laundry bleach and water before washing.

- Grass: Rub laundry detergent into stained area before washing. Add bleach if fabric is color-safe.

- Greasy butter, oil or food stains:Rub a bit of shampoo into the spot well, then rinse.

- Ink–ballpoint (method 1): Pour water through the stained area, then apply white vinegar, rubbing alcohol, or a stain removal product. Rinse thoroughly.

- Ink–ballpoint (method 2): Spray inky area with aerosol hair spray. Rub into stain, then launder as usual.

- Ink-felt tip: While felt pen marks are permanent, sometimes a stain can be removed by blotting the mark with a stain remover and washing the item in bleach, detergent, and very hot water.

- Jelly or Jam: Rinse in cold water, then soak stain in a solution of one tablespoon of white vinegar, 1/2 teaspoon liquid laundry detergent and 1 quart of warm water. Rinse, then launder.

- Lipstick: (See Ink-Ballpoint, method 2)

- Milk: Soak stain in cool water and laundry detergent, rinse and launder as usual.

- Motor oil, grease: Treat spot with laundry detergent or stain remover. Wash the item in the hottest water safe for the fabric.

- Mud: Brush off any loose or caked mud. Apply detergent to the spot and soak in cold water for 30 minutes, rubbing spot with a soft brush. Wash item in warm (not hot) water and detergent. Repeat if needed.

- Paint (water-based): Flush with warm water, then soak in a solution of one part dishwashing detergent to one part warm water. Sponge stain repeatedly until paint is removed.

- Paint (oil-based): Blot out as much paint as possible and rinse. With stain face down on an old towel, blot spot with turpentine, removing as much paint as possible. Soak spot overnight in solution of one part dishwashing detergent to one part warm water and launder.

LAUNDRY TIPS
Cleaning and Care

- Use white vinegar in your wash to cut down on suds.

- Throw a clean, colorfast tennis ball into your dryer to fluff towels, etc., and to cut drying time.

- Do not use fabric softener on your towels. Over time, softener builds up and lessens the absorbency of the towels.

- Clean your lint filter after EVERY load to cut down on fire risk.

- Wash your lint filter with dishwashing detergent and a stiff brush frequently, rinsing and drying before using again.

- To cut down on lint on your wash, add a cup of white vinegar to the final rinse cycle.

- If your machine overflows with suds, sprinkling salt will make the suds disappear.

- If your clothes are stiff, you are probably using too much detergent. Use no more than the recommended amount and add a cup of white vinegar to the rinse cycle.

- For spot removal or pre-soaking, skip harsh stain-removal products and bleach. Try white vinegar, table salt or baking soda on your stains first.

- Candle wax on your favorite tablecloth? Scrape off as much as possible, then sponge stain with dry cleaning solvent. Rinse, then launder the item.

- Candle wax (method 2): Scrape off as much as possible, then cover stain with newspaper or paper towel above AND below stain. Using a medium warm iron, heat the stained area, allowing extra wax to absorb into paper towel. Launder as usual.

- Keep your washer smelling fresh by leaving the door open between washes.

- Remove buildup from the bottom of your iron by scrubbing it with a paste of 1 part baking soda to 2 parts water. Use a clean damp cloth to wipe it off.

- Microfiber cleaning cloths should not be laundered with fabric softener. They'll lose their absorbent properties.

- Protect delicate washables by laundering them inside a pillowcase secured with a zip tie.

- If you run out of fabric softener, mix one part hair conditioner to three parts water and add it to your rinse cycle. Or dampen a washcloth with it and toss in the dryer.

- Dry knit items inside out to prevent pilling.

- If you forget to take your clothes out of the dryer and they're all wrinkled, throw in a damp towel and turn dryer on for 15 minutes. If more time is needed, continue drying, checking every 10 minutes until wrinkles are gone.

- If you accidentally mix colors with whites and tint your clothes, here's something to try. Mix 1/2 cup detergent, 1/2 cup salt and 1/2 cup baking soda in a tub of lukewarm water. Soak items until dye has been removed, then launder as usual.

- Save your used dryer sheets and give them a second life as a static-reducing dust cloth for your electronic devices.

CHAPTER 3

In the Kitchen

You don't need to use a calculator or log onto a computer to get frequently used measurement equivalents, roasting and freezing charts, good storage tips, and cooking substitutions—they're all right here! Plus, you'll find cooking tips on everything from remedying an over-spiced stew and fluffing up mashed potatoes.

With the Clever Chef in your corner, you'll be surprised how easy it is to whip up delicious meals sure to impress your family and guests. Look, too, at our money-saving suggestions for leftovers; and ways to perk up some old favorites. And time-strapped or not, who couldn't use a few clock-beating cooking tips? "In the Kitchen" will make cooking fun and easy for you and any and all your helpers, big and small!

COOKING MEASUREMENT EQUIVALENTS

1 tablespoon (tbsp) = 3 teaspoons (tsp)

1/16 cup =1 tablespoon

1/8 cup =2 tablespoons

1/6 cup =2 tablespoons + 2 teaspoons

1/4 cup = 4 tablespoons

1/3 cup = 5 tablespoons + 1 teaspoon

3/8 cup = 6 tablespoons

1/2 cup = 8 tablespoons

2/3 cup =10 tablespoons + 2 teaspoons

3/4 cup =12 tablespoons

1 cup = 48 teaspoons

1 cup = 16 tablespoons

8 fluid ounces (fl oz) = 1 cup

1 pint (pt) = 2 cups

1 quart (qt) = 2 pints

1 quart = 4 cups

1 gallon (gal) = 4 quarts

16 ounces (oz) = 1 pound (lb)

1 milliliter (ml) = 1 cubic centimeter (cc)

1 inch (in) = 2.54 centimeters (cm)

SMART TIPS FOR MEASURING

- Store measuring cups and spoons together in a one-gallon freezer bag so you can retrieve them quickly and easily.

- Never use your flatware spoons for measuring ingredients for recipes, because they will not give you an accurate measurement.

- Keep two sets of measuring spoons and cups—if you've just measured a liquid ingredient, you have a clean measure on hand for a dry ingredient.

- Be careful not to pack or press down on ingredients, unless the recipe calls for an ingredient to be lightly or firmly packed (as with shortening or brown sugar).

- Use a side dish when you level dry ingredients or pour liquids into spoons or cups; if you work over your mixing bowl, the excess will land in your mixture. Even a little too much flour, salt, water, or spices can affect the taste and texture of your food.

- Measure spices before you begin cooking so each will be ready for you to add at the right time.

ROASTING TEMPERATURES

Use of a meat thermometer recommended.

Internal Temperature   ° F

CASSEROLES

Beef, pork, veal, lamb 160

Turkey, Chicken 165

BEEF, VEAL, LAMB ROAST

Medium rare 145

Medium 160

Well-done 170

POULTRY

Chicken & Turkey, whole 165

Poultry breasts, roast 165

Poultry thighs, wings 165

Duck & goose 165

Pheasant 155

HAM

Raw 160

Pre-cooked 140

ROASTING TIMES

	Weight	Temp.	Cooking Time
BEEF			
Rib Roast, bone-in	4 to 6 lbs.	325	23 to 25 min. per lb.
Chuck Roast, brisket	3 to 4 lbs.	325	2 1/2 to 3 hrs.
Round or rump roast	2 1/2 to 4 lbs.	325	30 to 35 min. per lb.
Tenderloin, whole	4 to 6 lbs.	425	45 to 60 min. total
PORK			
Loin Roast	2 to 5 lbs.	325	20 to 30 min. per lb.
Crown Roast	4 to 6 lbs.	325	20 to 30 min. per lb.
Ham, fresh whole, bone-in	12 to 16 lbs.	325	18 to 20 min. per lb.
Ham, fresh half, bone-in	5 to 8 lbs.	325	22 to 25 min. per lb.
Shoulder or Butt roast	3 to 6 lbs.	325	35 to 40 min. per lb.
Tenderloin	1/2 to 1 1/2 lb.	425	20 to 30 min. total
Ribs	2 to 4 lbs.	325	1 1/2 to 2 hrs.
Loin Chops, bone-in	3/4" thick	350	6 to 8 min.
Loin Chops, boneless	1 1/2" thick	350	12 to 16 min.
CHICKEN			
Whole boiler fryer	3 to 4 lbs.	350	1 1/2 to 1 3/4 hrs.
Whole roasting hen	5 to 7 lbs.	350	2 to 2 1/4 hrs.
Breast halves, bone-in	6 to 8 oz.	350	30 to 40 min.
Breast half, boneless	4 oz.	350	20 to 30 min.
Legs or thighs	4 to 8 oz.	350	40 to 50 min.
Drumsticks	4 oz.	375	35 to 45 min.
Wings or wingettes	1 lb.	350	30 to 45 min.
TURKEY UNSTUFFED	4 to 6 lbs.(breast)	325	1 1/2 to 2 1/4 hrs.
	8 to 12 lbs.	325	2 3/4 to 3 hrs.
	12 to 14 lbs.	325	3 to 3 3/4 hrs.
TURKEY STUFFED	6 to 8 lbs. (breast)	325	2 1/2 to 3 1/2 hrs.
	8 to 12 lbs.	325	3 to 3 1/2 hrs.
	12 to 14 lbs.	325	3 1/2 to 4 lbs.

SMART TIPS FOR ROASTING

- For juicier baked chicken, start roasting the bird with the breast side down so juices permeate the breast meat. Finish roasting with breast side up.

- Allow 15-20 minutes for a roast to sit after you take it out of the oven. If you start slicing too soon, all the juices end up pooled on the serving plate rather than in the meat or poultry.

- Use an instant-read meat and poultry thermometer to avoid under- or over-cooking roasted food. When inserting the thermometer, make sure the tip doesn't touch a bone or settle in fat.

- Use sturdy tongs to turn or reposition the meat or poultry while roasting; a fork will cause juices to pool at the bottom of the pan and perhaps burn.

- Know the cut of meat you plan to use; different cuts call for different roasting methods (high heat vs. low heat, for example) and oven time.

- Set roast on a roasting rack inside the roasting pan, or set roast on top of a layer of vegetables, for even cooking.

- Invest in good-quality roasting pans to promote even cooking and reduce hard-to-clean sticking and burning.

FREEZER CHART

Recommended time limits are for maintaining flavor and texture.
NR - freezing not recommended.

Item	Months
BREADS & BAKED GOODS	
Cookies, muffins, breads	6-12
Unfrosted cakes	3
Fruit Pies	6-8
Pumpkin or chiffon pies	1-2
Unbaked rolls & breads	1
Cookie dough	3
DAIRY & EGGS	
Butter, margarine	9
Milk	1-3
Cheese, (cottage, ricotta, cream)	1
Cheese, (natural or processed)	6-8
Cream, light	1
Cream, heavy	NR
Ice cream, ice milk	2-4
Eggs, in shell	NR
FRUITS	
Home frozen	10
Canned fruits, opened	2
Juices	12
Citrus fruits	4-6
VEGETABLES	
Home frozen	10
Purchased frozen	8
MEAT, ROASTS, STEAKS, CHOPS	
Beef	6-12
Veal, pork	4-9
Lamb	6-9

Item	Months
Ground meats, stew meat	3-4
Sausage	1-2
Cooked meat dishes	2-3
Gravy & broth	2-3
Canned, opened	NR
Soups, stews	4-6
MEAT, PROCCESSED & CURED	
Bacon	1
Frankfurters	1-2
Ham (whole, half)	1-2
Ham (canned, unopened)	NR
Luncheon Meats	1-2
POULTRY, FRESH	
Chicken, turkey (whole)	12
Chicken, turkey (pieces)	6 8
Duck, goose (whole)	6
POULTRY, COOKED	
Cooked poultry dishes	1-6
Pieces in broth	6
Pieces not in broth	1
Fried chicken	4
SEAFOOD	
Clams, oysters, scallops	3-4
Crab	2
Shrimp, lobster	6-12
Freshwater fish	6-9
Fillets	4-6
Salmon steaks	2
Cooked fish	1

SMART TIPS FOR FREEZING

- Divide ground meat into several small sections before freezing. That way, you can use a portion of the meat without needing to thaw the whole amount. And, if you want the whole amount, the meat will thaw faster in small sections.

- Wrap steaks and chops individually to avoid freezer burn.

- Trim excess fat from meats before freezing to avoid rancidity.

- Thaw frozen fish fillets in milk to restore that fresh-caught flavor.

- Leftover rice can be kept in the freezer for up to 6 months. Make sure container is tightly covered.

- Freeze lemon juice, sauces, and broth in ice cube trays or small, sealable plastic bags for use in stews, soups, and casseroles.

- Keep empty butter wrappers in freezer to use when coating baking dishes or muffin tins.

FOOD STORAGE TIPS

- Keep lettuce and leafy greens crisp by wrapping leaves loosely in damp paper towels and refrigerating in a sealed plastic bag.

- Wrap fresh celery in aluminum foil to retain freshness longer. Refrigerate.

- Place elevated wire racks at the back of cupboards so you can easily see stored canned goods.

- Store herbs and spices in a cool, dry, dark place to preserve freshness.

- Store flour, sugar, rice, pasta, cereal, and all bulk foods in waterproof, bug- and rodent-proof glass, tin, or food-grade plastic containers.

- Keep freshly cut basil in a glass with enough water to cover only the stems; set on kitchen counter.

FOOD STORAGE TIPS

- Keep asparagus fresh by standing stalks upright in a glass of water. Refrigerate.

- Coat exposed edges of cheese with butter to retard drying and hardening.

- Place an apple in a bag of potatoes to keep them from budding while stored.

- Store tomatoes stem-side down in a cool place to help keep them from over-ripening.

- Ripen green fruit in a paper bag, or in a perforated plastic bag. Check daily.

- Pack lettuce, tomato slices, and pickles separately from sandwiches when preparing sack lunches and picnic fare to avoid soggy bread. Assemble when ready to eat.

- Purée over-ripe apples, strawberries, and tomatoes, then freeze for use in meal, dessert, and beverage recipes.

- Store brown sugar in an air-tight glass jar in a cool place. To soften hardened sugar, place a slice of bread in the jar overnight.

FOOD STORAGE TIPS

- Keep the root half, not the top half, of an onion for later use; it will stay fresher longer than the top.

- Store ripened fruit in the refrigerator to retain sweetness longer; keep grapes in a perforated plastic wrap.

- Refrigerate fresh corn; leave unhusked.

- Refrigerate freshly cooked foods within two hours to avoid spoilage.

- Store food items away from non-food items, particularly soap, fuel, and insecticides, to avoid possible odor seepage or contamination.

- Store olive oil in a cool, dark spot away from a heat or light source. Keep the jar tightly covered, as air will cause it to go rancid. If oil clouds, it has gotten too cold and will clear after it has warmed.

- Wrap sandwich bread, soft rolls, and buns in a tightly closed plastic bag. Leave French bread and sourdough bread unwrapped or lightly covered to retain crispy crust.

FOOD STORAGE TIPS

- Keep your pantry up-to-date by stacking newly purchased items to the back and pulling older items forward to use first.

- Store leafy greens and seeded fruits and vegetables separately to preserve freshness of the greens.

- Store carrots and apples separately to avoid bitter-tasting carrots.

- Store potatoes and onions separately to keep potatoes from turning bad.

COOKING SUBSTITUTIONS
for Many Common Ingredients

Allspice (1 tsp):
1/2 tsp cinnamon + 1/4 tsp ginger + 1/4 tsp ground cloves

Apple Pie Spice (1 Tbsp):
2 tsp ground cinnamon + 1 tsp ground nutmeg + 1/8 tsp allspice

Arugula: baby spinach

Baking Powder (1 tsp double-acting):
1/4 tsp baking soda + 1/2 cup buttermilk OR
1/4 tsp baking soda + 1/2 tsp cream of tartar

Balsamic Vinegar (1 Tbsp):
1 Tbsp red wine or cider vinegar + 1/2 tsp sugar

Barbeque Sauce (1 cup):
1 cup catsup + 1/2 tsp liquid smoke + 1/4 cup brown sugar

Bouquet Garni (1 tsp):
1/2 tsp dried parsley +1/2 tsp dried thyme + 1 crushed bay leaf

Bread Crumbs (fine, dry), 1/2 cup:
1/2 cup cracker crumbs or 1/2 cup cornflake crumbs

Broth, Chicken or Beef (1 cup):
1 tsp bouillon granules or 1 bouillon cube,
dissolved in 1 cup boiling water

COOKING SUBSTITUTIONS
for Many Common Ingredients

Butter (1 cup):
1 cup margarine OR 7/8 cup lard + 1/2 tsp salt

Buttermilk (1 cup):
1 Tbsp vinegar + sweet milk to equal 1 cup OR
2/3 cup plain yogurt + 1/3 cup sweet milk

Butternut Squash (1 cup cooked):
1 cup canned pumpkin purée

Cardamom (1 tsp):
1/2 tsp cinnamon + 1/4 tsp ground cloves + 1/4 tsp nutmeg

Catsup (1 cup):
1 cup tomato sauce + 1/2 cup sugar + 2 Tbsp white vinegar

Chili Powder (1-1/2 tsp):
1 tsp hot pepper sauce + 1/4 tsp each oregano and cumin

Chocolate (1 ounce):
3 Tbsp cocoa + 1 Tbsp shortening

Cocktail Sauce (1/2 cup):
1/2 cup catsup + 1 tsp prepared horseradish

Cornstarch (1 Tbsp): 2 Tbsp flour

COOKING SUBSTITUTIONS
for Many Common Ingredients

Cream, heavy (1 cup):
1/3 cup butter + 3/4 cup milk

Currants (1 cup): 1 cup raisins

Dates, pitted (1 cup): 1 cup dried figs or raisins

Dill (1 tsp): 1 tsp tarragon

Eggs (1 large): 1/4 cup egg substitute

Eggplant: zucchini

Evaporated Milk (1 cup): 1 cup light cream

Fats for baking (1 cup): 1 cup applesauce

Flour, All-Purpose (1 cup): 1 cup + 2 Tbsp cake flour

Flour, Cake (1 cup): 7/8 cup all-purpose flour

Flour, Self-Rising (1 cup):
1 cup all-purpose flour + 1-1/2 tsp baking powder + 1/4 tsp salt

Garlic (1 small clove): 1/8 tsp garlic powder

Ginger, fresh grated (1 tsp): 1/4 tsp ground ginger

COOKING SUBSTITUTIONS
for Many Common Ingredients

Half and Half (1 cup):
1 Tbsp melted butter or margarine + whole milk to equal 1 cup

Herbs, fresh snipped (1 Tbsp):
1/2 to 1 tsp dried herb, crushed; or 1/2 tsp ground

Honey (1 cup):
1-1/4 cup granulated sugar + 1/4 cup of additional liquid already in recipe

Hot Pepper Sauce (1 tsp):
3/4 tsp cayenne pepper + 1 tsp white vinegar

Italian Seasoning (1 tsp):
1/2 tsp dried oregano + 1/4 tsp dried thyme + 1/4 tsp dried basil

Jicama: water chestnuts, drained

Kale: collard greens, turnip greens or spinach

Key Limes: Persian limes (regular grocery limes)

Leeks: equal amount chopped green onion

Lemon Grass (2 stalks): zest from 1 lemon

Lemon Juice (1 Tbsp): 1 Tbsp distilled white vinegar

COOKING SUBSTITUTIONS
for Many Common Ingredients

Maple Syrup (1 cup):
3/4 cup light corn syrup + 1/4 cup butter + 1/2 tsp maple extract

Mayonnaise (1 cup):
1 cup sour cream or 1 cup plain yogurt

Milk, fresh whole (1 cup):
1 cup reconstituted dry milk + 2 tsp butter

Molasses (1 cup): 1 cup honey

Mushrooms, fresh (1 cup):
4-oz jar or can mushroom stems and pieces

Mustard, dry (1 tsp): 1 Tbsp prepared mustard

Nutmeg (1 tsp): 1 tsp allspice or ground mace

Onion, chopped (1/2 cup): 1/2 tsp onion powder

Orzo (1 cup cooked): 1 cup cooked rice

Pine Nuts: equal amounts walnuts or pecans, chopped

Poultry Seasoning (1 tsp):
3/4 tsp crushed dried sage + 1/4 tsp marjoram and/or thyme

COOKING SUBSTITUTIONS
for Many Common Ingredients

Pumpkin Pie Spice (1 tsp):
1/2 tsp cinnamon + 1/4 tsp ginger + 1/4 tsp ground cloves + 1/8 tsp nutmeg

Quinoa (1 cup): 1 cup couscous or bulgur

Raisins (1/2 cup):
1/2 cup minced, pitted prunes or dates

Rice, white (1 cup):
1 cup cooked barley or bulgur

Ricotta Cheese (1 cup):
1 cup silken tofu or dry curd cottage cheese

Saffron (1/4 tsp): 1/4 tsp turmeric

Shallots, chopped (1/2 cup):
1/2 cup of chopped onion, or chopped green onion

Sour Cream (1 cup): 1 cup plain yogurt

Sugar, brown (1 cup):
3/4 cup granulated sugar + 1/4 cup molasses

Sugar, Powdered (1 1/3 cups): 1 cup granulated sugar

COOKING SUBSTITUTIONS
for Many Common Ingredients

Sweetened Condensed Milk (14 oz):
3/4 cup sugar + 1/2 cup water + 1 1/8 cup dried
powdered milk; brought to boil and stirred
frequently until thick (about 20 min)

Taco Seasoning (1 Tbsp):
2 tsp chili powder + 1/4 tsp dried oregano + 1/4 tsp cumin
+ 1/8 tsp each garlic and onion powder + 1/4 tsp salt

Tartar Sauce (1/2 cup):
6 Tbsp mayonnaise + 2 Tbsp pickle relish

Tomato Juice (1 cup):
1/2 cup tomato sauce + 1/2 cup water

Vegetable Shortening (1 cup):
1 cup + 2 Tbsp unsalted butter

Vinegar (1 tsp): 1 tsp lemon or lime juice

Wasabi (1 Tbsp):
1 Tbsp prepared horseradish, drained + 1 tsp dried mustard
+ 1 tsp water (mix together and let rest for 15 min before serving)

COOKING SUBSTITUTIONS
for Many Common Ingredients

Worcestershire Sauce (1 Tbsp):
2 tsp soy sauce + 4 drops hot pepper sauce
+ 1/4 tsp lemon juice + 1/4 tsp granulated sugar

Yellow Squash: zucchini or pattypan squash

Yogurt (1 cup): 1 cup silken tofu (blended) OR sour cream

Zest of Lemon (1/2 tsp): 1/2 tsp lemon extract

Zucchini: yellow squash

Calorie-Cutting
SUBSTITUTIONS

- Reduce the amount of Cheddar cheese; substitute Parmesan cheese.

- Use low-fat chicken broth instead of butter and milk when fixing mashed potatoes.

Calorie-Cutting
SUBSTITUTIONS

- Remove skin from chicken before cooking.

- Sauté food in broth or stock instead of oil.

- Use less butter, oil, shortening, and sugar in recipes where possible.

- Replace, or partially substitute, butter or oil with fat-free sour cream, applesauce, light cream cheese, fruit purée, or juice.

- Use ground turkey instead of ground beef in lasagna, sloppy joes, pizzas, and casseroles.

- Use vegetables—mushrooms, spinach, carrots, peas—instead of ground meat or sausage in lasagna and casseroles.

- Mix mayonnaise with low-fat plain yogurt for tuna, chicken, and egg salad dishes.

- Use low-fat or fat-free products where possible.

Calorie-Cutting
SUBSTITUTIONS

- Avoid using oil in frying with non-stick cooking spray or non-stick pans.

- Top salads with low-fat mozzarella cheese and low-fat dressing.

- Choose low-fat dairy products.

- Substitute evaporated milk for cream in recipes.

- Thicken soups, stews, sauces, and gravy with puréed vegetables instead of flour or heavy cream.

- Rely on herbs and spices rather than on oils for flavor.

- Dip a slice of bread into soups and stews to remove grease

Handy
COOKING TIPS

- Add salt to water used for boiling—food will cook faster because the water will boil at a higher temperature.

- Keep mashed potatoes warm in a slow cooker until serving time.

- Pass gravy through a strainer to remove lumps.

- Thicken gravy with 1 tablespoon of cornstarch; or 2 tablespoons of flour; or puréed vegetables.

- Add a pinch of baking soda to gravy if it seems too greasy.

- Snip fresh herbs with kitchen scissors rather than chop them with a knife.

- Use unflavored dental floss to get neat, clean slices of soft cheese, cheesecake, and rolled dough.

- Soften butter quickly by cutting into pats, putting them in a bowl, and sitting bowl in warm water.

Handy
COOKING TIPS

- Grate fresh Parmesan cheese on pasta after draining to help sauce stick.

- Add a bay leaf to the water when boiling cabbage to reduce smell.

- Chill bowl and beaters before whipping cream for fluffier whipped cream.

- Pour gravy that has been burned into another pan and add a little sugar to counteract burned taste; continue to cook.

- Place a slice of white bread on top of burned rice to absorb burned taste.

- Leave a little space between tidbits stacked on kabob skewers. That way, pieces cook evenly and basting sauce reaches all sides.

- Prevent sticky lids by putting a piece of plastic wrap over the jar or bottle before screwing the lid back on.

Handy
COOKING TIPS

- Marinate chicken no longer than the time specified in recipe to avoid mushiness.

- Dip tomatoes, peaches, and pears in hot water for several seconds for easier peeling.

- Restore loose whipped cream by stirring in an egg white. Chill, then re-beat.

- Handle hamburger patties as little as possible to retain tenderness and juiciness.

- Wash strawberries in cold running water to keep them firm.

- Let hot tea cool before putting it in the refrigerator for ice tea to avoid clouding.

- Peel bananas from the bottom to avoid leaving strings behind.

- Cook beans until they're tender before you add seasonings and other ingredients to avoid toughening the beans.

Handy
COOKING TIPS

- Separate bananas to slow ripening process.

- Keep oil or butter from burning in the frying pan by adding a dab of oil to butter, or a dab of butter to oil.

- Keep rice from boiling over by rimming the pan with butter or grease.

- Cook broth, soups, and stews the day before and store overnight in the refrigerator. The fat will rise to the top and you can easily skim it off when ready to reheat.

- Check freshness of baking powder by adding one teaspoon of powder to about 1/3 cup water. If the water doesn't fizz, the baking powder is old.

- Bring out the flavor of chopped nuts by lightly roasting them before adding to cookie and cake recipes and salads.

- Prevent cookie dough from spreading in hot or humid weather by chilling it in the refrigerator for 15 minutes before spooning out and baking.

Handy
COOKING TIPS

- Use a sheet of parchment paper instead of butter or oil to grease a cookie sheet. Cookies won't stick and clean-up is easier.

- Fix lopsided cake layers by removing the top with a length of dental floss. Flip the layer bottom side up.

Clever Chef
BREAKFAST
Tips & Cooking Secrets

- Bake your bacon, instead of frying. Place it on a baking sheet and roast at 375 degrees for 10-15 minutes, until crisp.

- For perfect French toast, add a pinch of brown sugar, salt and cinnamon to the butter in the pan. Add bread when butter foams.

- Try adding a bit of cream cheese while scrambling eggs for a richer flavor.

- Add a tablespoon of vinegar to the pot while making hard-boiled eggs. They'll peel easier.

- Roll sausage patties in flour before browning to prevent them from splitting and to reduce splatter.

- To easily separate eggs, use a funnel. The white goes through and the yolk stays intact in the funnel.

- Adding a pinch of cornstarch before beating the eggs yields fluffier omelets.

- Use cold coffee instead of milk to add a boost to your morning smoothie.

- Freeze overripe banana slices on a cookie sheet until frozen, then store slices in freezer bags. You'll be able to easily pull out just what you need for smoothies.

- To tell the difference between a fresh and hard-boiled egg, spin it on the counter. If it spins easily, it's cooked; if wobbly, it is raw.

- Hard-boiled eggs slice easier when you dip the knife blade in water before cutting.

- For an easy egg breakfast, spray a microwave-safe 12 oz. mug with cooking spray. Crack in an egg and a tablespoon of milk, plus salt and pepper. Mix with fork, then microwave on High for 30-45 seconds. Remove and stir again, cook for an additional 30-45 seconds. Slide onto a toasted English muffin or toast.

- Create more nutritious pancakes by adding reduced-fat yogurt instead of water in the batter.

- After ladling batter onto griddle for pancakes, sprinkle granola over the batter.

Clever Chef
BREAKFAST
Tips & Cooking Secrets

- For easy vanilla coffee creamer, mix 1 can of sweetened condensed milk, 2 cups of milk and 1 1/2 teaspoons of high-quality vanilla. Store in fridge up to a week.

- Out of syrup? Try heating applesauce with cinnamon and ladling it over waffles and pancakes.

- Add dried cherries and blueberries while making cooked oatmeal. They'll add plump juiciness without added sugar.

- Do not over-beat muffin batter. Stir until barely blended and you'll get more rounded muffins.

SMART TIPS FOR BREAKFAST TASKS

- Bring egg whites to room temperature for best volume. Beat just until desired stiffness. Using a large whisk or slotted spoon, gently blend whites into mixture until no streaks remain.

- Bring eggs to room temperature before boiling to avoid cracked shells. Rinse in cold water after cooking for easy peeling.

- Test egg freshness by immersing the egg in a pan of salted water. If the egg sinks, it's good; but if it bobs to the surface, it's bad.

- Use an ice cream scoop to pour pancake batter onto the griddle; fillings into mini pie shells; batter into muffin tins.

- Get more juice from oranges and lemons by microwaving for about 30 seconds; or sitting them in hot water for about 15 minutes.

Clever Chef
LUNCH
Tips & Cooking Secrets

- Adding rinds of cheeses like Parmesan to broths and soups adds rich flavor.

- Using Greek yogurt for half the mayo in a salad dressing recipe cuts fat and adds tang.

- Brighten up the flavor of split pea soup by stirring in a cup of frozen peas a few minutes before serving.

- Easy deviled eggs: after boiling, place yolks and other ingredients into a plastic bag and smash together. Cut a tip off the corner and squeeze contents into whites.

- Let carrot sticks soak in pickle juice overnight to give them a zesty flavor.

- Soak limp produce in ice water to restore crispness.

- Spice up your coleslaw or salad dressing by adding leftover juice from pickled jalapenos or spicy pickles.

- Freeze pesto in ice cube trays, then store in freezer bags to add individually to sauces and soup.

Clever Chef
LUNCH
Tips & Cooking Secrets

- If you accidentally over-salt a soup or sauce, adding sliced raw potato will absorb some of it. Remove before serving.

- Adding leftover vegetables and slightly wilted greens to tomato juice and water makes a delicious, economical soup.

- Wrap a clean brick in aluminum foil and place it on top of sandwiches when grilling for faster, even browning.

- Cottage cheese and sour cream will keep better if stored upside down in the fridge.

- Save extra cooked pasta in a plastic bag and store in the fridge. Place the pasta in boiling water for about 30 seconds and serve.

- To help slice a tomato evenly, prick the side with a fork and use the marks as a cutting guide.

Clever Chef
LUNCH
Tips & Cooking Secrets

- Make a lower calorie creamy soup by adding a few teaspoons of instant mashed potato flakes to simmering vegetables and stock. Purée before serving.

- When making sandwiches, spread mayo or butter all the way to the edges to help prevent sogginess.

- Chill your serving plates to keep your salad crisp longer.

- Dark greens are much more nutritious than iceberg lettuce.

- For easy cleanup, try mixing your burger ingredients in a zip-top plastic bag. Knead until combined. Store unused mixture in the freezer.

- Cut up a rotisserie chicken and combine it with your favorite bottled barbeque sauce. Heat and serve for easy pulled chicken sandwiches.

DINNER
Tips & Cooking Secrets

- Before you roast a whole chicken, lay whole stalks of rosemary and/or sage on the roasting rack.

- A little salt on your cutting board keeps herbs in their place while you chop them.

- Plunging the steamed stalks into ice water will produce broccoli with a bright emerald color.

- Do not add oil to the water when cooking pasta. The sauce will not stick properly.

- Pat meat and fish dry before cooking to cut down on splatter and make browning easier.

- Tone down spiciness in a recipe by adding a dash of lemon juice.

- Substitute instant potatoes instead of breadcrumbs in breaded fish and chicken dishes.

- To peel garlic easily, place cloves in the microwave for 15 seconds. The skins will come right off.

Clever Chef
DINNER
Tips & Cooking Secrets

- Make your own herbed butter by mixing chopped garlic, salt and fresh chopped herbs into softened butter. Add to breads and sauces. It's great on popcorn too!

- Use a damp, clean sponge or paper towel to clean mushrooms. They soak up too much water under the faucet.

- Add more brown color to your gravy by stirring in a sprinkle of instant coffee.

- A roast with the bone in will cook faster than boneless, as the bone conducts heat.

- Instead of a roasting rack, place your roast or chicken on top of a stack of carrots, celery and onion in the roasting pan. The fat will drip through and the drippings will have much more flavor.

- Remove silk from fresh corn with a dampened paper towel. Brush downward.

Clever Chef
DINNER
Tips & Cooking Secrets

- To reduce the acidity when making spaghetti sauce, try adding a spoonful of grape jelly.

- Thaw frozen fish fillets in milk to give them a fresher taste.

- To minimize lumpiness, always add hot or warm milk when mashing potatoes.

- To make a ham less salty, bake for half the allotted time, and then drain the juices. Pour a cup or two of ginger ale over the ham and bake till done.

- Adding a small amount of vinegar to cooking cabbage will absorb some of the odor.

- Mushrooms won't get slimy if you wrap them in paper towels before refrigerating.

Clever Chef
DESSERTS
Tips & Cooking Secrets

- To peel ginger, use the edge of a teaspoon and scrape it around the edges.

- A dash of aged balsamic vinegar enhances the flavor of strawberries.

- Store whole gingerroot in the freezer. Grating will be much easier.

- Revive dried out coconut flakes by sprinkling them with milk. Let stand 5-10 minutes before using.

- If your brown sugar is rock hard and you don't have time to soften it, grate the amount you need with a box grater.

- Instead of using flour to dust pans, use cocoa powder when baking a chocolate cake or brownies.

- To slice a cake into two layers, first place 6-8 toothpicks around the edge to mark the halfway point, then take unflavored dental floss, and wrap it around the cake above the picks. Cross the ends and pull to slice.

Clever Chef
DESSERTS
Tips & Cooking Secrets

- Transform instant chocolate pudding into mousse by substituting whipping cream for the water.

- If you whip store-bought canned frosting with your electric mixer, you'll have lighter, fluffier topping for your cake, and increased volume to make frosting go further.

- Spray a measuring cup with cooking spray before measuring molasses, syrup or honey and it will slide out easier.

- Toss blueberries lightly with flour in a paper bag before adding to your cake or muffin recipe.

- Use your ice cream scoop to fill muffin and cupcake tins.

- Brush beaten egg white over the top crust before baking your pie for a glossy pastry finish.

- Hull fresh strawberries by pushing a strong plastic straw through the bottom and up through the top.

Clever Chef
DESSERTS
Tips & Cooking Secrets

- Cut your brownies and bars into squares with your pizza cutter.

- Roll piecrusts between 2 sheets of parchment paper or waxed paper. Using less flour will result in more tender pastry.

- Place a mini marshmallow into the bottom of your sugar cone to keep ice cream from dripping out the bottom.

- To quickly bring butter to room temperature, use a box grater and shred it into your mixing bowl.

Don't Throw It Away—
USE IT UP!

AVOCADOS
Turn mushy avocados into a tasty guacamole dip. In a bowl, mash avocados. Stir in chopped tomato, if desired. Add to taste: lemon or lime juice, cilantro, onion, garlic, salt. Grab the leftover chips or crackers, and enjoy a festive snack any day!

BANANAS
- Ripe bananas can be stored for up to two weeks in the refrigerator. While the skin will darken, the fruit should remain tasty.

- Dip or roll ripe bananas in chocolate syrup and freeze for later use.

- Over-ripe bananas can be chopped and frozen for later use in banana bread recipes or in smoothies, or eaten as is as a frozen snack.

BREAD
Cut stale bread into cubes.
- Toss cubes in melted butter and seasonings to taste; bake in low oven (200°) for 45-50 minutes. Use as croutons in soups and salads.

Don't Throw It Away—
USE IT UP!

BREAD
Cut stale bread into cubes.
- Use cubes in bread pudding.

- Mix with chopped onion and celery, season to taste, and use for stuffing in chicken, turkey, or pork dishes.

- Bake cubes in low oven until crispy. Make breadcrumbs by pouring cubes into a clean plastic bag and crushing with a rolling pin.

BUNS
Put "orphaned" hot dog, hamburger, or hoagie buns in the freezer. To use, thaw buns slightly; spread with butter and top with Parmesan or cheddar cheese. Broil until toasty.

CAKE
They'll never know it's more than a day old if it's under ice cream, whipped topping, pudding or custard. Cube cake into bite-sized pieces, add fruit or preserves if desired, and scoop on favorite topping.

CEREAL
Most any dry breakfast cereal can be used as a coating for baked chicken. First dip chicken pieces in beaten egg, then dredge through crushed cereal. Bake as usual.

Don't Throw It Away—
USE IT UP!

CHICKEN
You're in luck if you have leftover chicken. Chop it up for sandwiches, salads, omelets, casseroles, tortilla rolls, pasta sauce.

COOKIES AND CRACKERS
- Crush stale cookies and sprinkle over pudding or ice cream.

- Crush stale crackers over creamy noodle dishes, such as macaroni and cheese.

- Use cracker crumbs in meat loaf.

- Revive soggy cookies or crackers by heating in oven at 350° until dry.

- Create a refrigerator cake by layering cookies (or cake strips) with pudding and whipped topping. Chill.

- Make ice cream sandwiches with graham crackers or thin cookies. Slice ice cream into 1/2 inch slices, sized to the cookies or crackers being used, and make the sandwich. Serve immediately or wrap and freeze.

Don't Throw It Away—
USE IT UP!

DINNER LEFTOVERS

Anything Goes! Pizza
Whatever you have, it will work!

Select for the base: Prepared pizza crust, Italian bread shell, sour dough bread slices, English muffins, flatbread.
Select for the topping: sliced or chopped onions; chopped peppers; vegetables; chopped meat or chicken; mushrooms; olives; shredded Swiss cheese, Parmesan cheese, or Mozzarella cheese.
Select for the sauce: 1 can pizza sauce, or make your own tangy sauce by boiling chopped onion and peppers in a small amount of water for 3-4 minutes until tender. Drain. Stir about 2 tablespoons of mustard. Spread over base, add toppings and cheese.
Bake at 400° for 10-15 minutes, or until cheese is bubbling.

EGGS
- When eggs are getting close to expiration date, use them up in egg-rich dishes such as omelets, soufflé, quiche, custards, bread pudding, angel cake.

- Use up hard-cooked eggs in casseroles, salads, and salad dressing.

Don't Throw It Away—
USE IT UP!

LEMONS

- Slice and freeze for later use in water or iced tea.

- After cooking, rub lemon on fingers to get rid of onion and garlic odors.

Handy Hint: Just a slice or two of a lemon, lime, or orange makes a decoration for beverage glasses, salads, and desserts. Cut a thin slice of citrus fruit, then cut from one edge to the center of the slice. Twist ends in opposite directions. If you have two kinds of fruit, twist two slices together.

MASHED POTATOES

- Stir leftover mashed potatoes into pancake batter and fry as usual.

- Use mashed potatoes in place of flour or cornstarch to thicken broth for soup.

- Spoon potatoes on top of stew, sprinkle with Parmesan cheese, and heat.

- Add a beaten egg, a tablespoon of flour, grated onion, salt, and pepper to taste. Form into patty and fry. Optional: add grated cheddar cheese to mix.

Don't Throw It Away—
USE IT UP!

MEATS

- Boil meat bones along with sliced onion, carrots, and seasonings to taste for delicious homemade broth. Use broth instead of water when boiling rice for extra flavor. Freeze for later use in soups and stews.

- Use up a small amount of beef or pork by stirring it into canned baked beans. Heat, and pour over a bun, toast, or cornbread.

- Chop leftover slices of meatloaf for tacos, burritos, sloppy joes, or most any other recipe calling for ground beef.

- Before you thaw frozen eye of round roast or thick steak, cut off paper-thin slices and pound slices with a meat mallet. Stir fry meat in a bit of oil. Add vegetables on hand, such as spinach, broccoli, peppers, onions, carrots. Splash with a little broth and soy sauce to taste, and serve over rice for an economical Chinese-inspired meal.

- Use up uncooked beef, pork, or chicken by making kabobs for dinner. On skewers, thread bite-sized meat or poultry chunks along with chunks of fruit or vegetables. Brush with soy sauce, BBQ sauce, mustard, ketchup, or Worcester sauce, if desired. Grill or broil. Serve with rice.

Don't Throw It Away—
USE IT UP!

NOODLES

- Add broth and leftover vegetables for a delicious next-day soup.

- Marinate in salad dressing. Add leftover veggies, chopped meat or poultry, tomato, and hard-cooked egg. Toss and chill. Toss again before serving.

PASTA

Mix leftover noodles or cut-up spaghetti with leftover vegetables and cooked meat. Stir in a can of cream soup (such as chicken, mushroom, or cheddar cheese). Heat and enjoy.

PEPPERS

When the summer garden overflows with green, red, and yellow peppers, freeze them for use all winter long. Cut, core, and remove seeds. Slice or dice, as desired. Blanch, then seal in zippered bags and store in freezer.

PIE CRUST LEFTOVERS

Make sweet and tasty pie crust morsels with left over dough. Roll it out, slather with butter, sprinkle with cinnamon and sugar. Starting at the long edge, roll the dough jellyroll-style, then cut into bite-sized pieces. Bake until slightly browned.

Don't Throw It Away—
USE IT UP!

SALAD DRESSING
- Spread on lunchmeat sandwiches and hamburger patties for tangy flavor.

- Use along with mayonnaise when mixing tuna salad sandwiches.

- Add a small amount of salad dressing to deviled eggs.

- Use alone, or combine with a dab of mustard and use as a marinade for chicken, pork, or seafood.

TOMATOES
When summer's bounty provides you with more tomatoes than you can eat at one time, try this: In a large pot, boil whole, unpeeled tomatoes for one minute. Remove from water and let cool. Remove skin and core, seal in bag or container, and freeze. Use later in winter-time soups, stews, and savory skillet dinners.

TORTILLAS
- Tear apart or cut into pieces. Spray cookie sheet with cooking spray and spread out tortilla pieces. Bake until crisp. Eat with salsa for a tasty snack.

Don't Throw It Away—
USE IT UP!

TORTILLAS
- Warm. Serve as an edible scoop with thick soup, chili, and stew.

- Tear apart. Use as the bottom layer for ground beef and tomato casserole.

VEGETABLES
- Place cooked vegetables in a container in the freezer and add to it over the course of several weeks. Use in soups, stews, curries, casseroles, rice pilaf.

- Purée cooked vegetables and use for flavor and thickening in soups and stews.

- Shred raw carrots over salads or cottage cheese for added flavor and crunch—and a few extra vitamins.

- Cut up leftover vegetables and add them to your next lasagna, meat pie, quiche, pizza, or quesadilla.

- Use yesterday's cooked vegetables, along with shredded cheese or sour cream, as topping for today's baked potato.

ZUCCHINI
- Grate or chop and add to salads.
- Add shredded zucchini to meatloaf mixture.

Time-Saving
TIPS!

- Keep a supply of paper plates and plastic flatware to use when dinner is a 15-minute affair between meetings, games, events, and classes.

- Make extra cookie dough and freeze half to use next time (dough will keep for about three months in the freezer).

- Make extra pancakes or waffles. Stack them with a piece of aluminum foil between each one; wrap in a plastic bag; freeze. When needed for a quick breakfast, they can be heated in the microwave for a minute or so.

- Cook in bulk whenever possible; freeze unused portions for later.

- Boil vegetables along with noodles or macaroni; drain everything together and serve.

- Plan meals several days or a week in advance. Cook ahead, and either refrigerate or freeze.

- Keep a current stock of ingredients and products that you use frequently to avoid a last-minute dash to the store.

Time-Saving
TIPS!

- Cook enough meat or poultry for two or three dinners. Vary the meals by changing sauces or side dishes.

- Organize the contents of kitchen cabinets and drawers. Keep similar items together so you can find them quickly; and most-used items conveniently located. Free-up counter space by storing infrequently used appliances.

- Set up a safe place in the kitchen where tots can "help" with child-sized cooking tasks; it will keep them occupied and away from hot stoves and ovens.

- Buy prepared foods that are healthy and truly save time, such as canned beans or frozen vegetables.

- Eat unpeeled fruits and vegetables—you'll save time and gain the nutrients and fiber in the skin.

- Focus on one-pot and slow-cooker recipes. You'll have easy-to-prepare savory meals with minimum clean-up.

- Get the next day's meals planned and all ingredients together and prepared as far as possible. After a long day, all you need to do is assemble and cook.

Kitchen
ZINGERS

NO MORE SAME-OLD, SAME-OLD
In meat loaf, substitute seasoned croutons or stuffing mix for bread crumbs to give the old standby an extra zing.

OLÉ!
Use an envelope of taco seasoning to add zest to hamburger patties, meat loaf, vegetable dips, casseroles, slow-cooker recipes, and stews.

STIR FRY SURPRISE
To give your next stir-fry meal a little twist, stir in eggs; add peanuts or cashews; add slivers of orange peel; substitute tofu for meat.

BUENO!
For popcorn with south-of-the-border zing, try this: To a bowl of warm popcorn, add a mixture of taco seasoning, melted butter, and cheddar cheese. Mix and eat!

POTATO PIZAZZ
So you think mashed potatoes are dull? Add Pizazz with a dollop or two of sour cream or softened cream cheese; season with paprika; sprinkle with Parmesan cheese.

POTATO BAKE
Many leftovers make great potato toppings! Particularly tasty are chili; stew; gravy (add vegetables, plus tuna or chicken); chopped ham and grated cheese; salsa, hamburger meat and grated cheese; taco filling and grated cheese.

GRILL-ICIOUS!
Top pork chops or fish fillets with salsa or chopped onions and pepper while grilling for extra pizzazz.

TASTY TUNA
Add finely chopped nuts, oranges, apples, or olives; small berries; pesto; or bacon bits for a terrific tuna sandwich.

THAT'S USING YOUR NOODLE!
Spice up plain noodles with a sauce using a cup of chicken or beef broth, thickened with flour or cornstarch. Flavor with curry powder, oregano, ginger, cilantro, paprika. Add chopped onions and peppers; mixed vegetables, chopped; nuts; crushed or diced tomatoes; mushrooms.

CHEERS FOR CHIPOTLE
Perk up the taste buds by adding a can of chipotle chiles to stew, soup, rice, or casseroles.

CHAPTER 4

Practical and Painless Money-Saving Tips

You can save a surprising amount of money by making a few small adjustments in your spending habits. If you're like most of us, you think nothing of picking up a cup of coffee, a can of soda, or convenient snack several times a week. Yet if you figure what you spend each month on these small purchases, you realize they're hardly "small" at all!

In this section, you'll discover painless ways to trim the amount you spend on clothes, entertainment, and shopping. You'll learn what you can do around the house to lessen utility bills and minimize upkeep and repair costs, as well as how to reduce transportation and travel expenses. Last but far from least, you'll find a list of guidelines for lasting financial stability in Thrifty Living.

A little *change* now can add up to big *dollars* later!

FOOD AND BEVERAGES

- Plan the week's menu around what's on sale at the grocery store. Look at ads in store flyers or online; clip or print coupons.

- Shop with a list to avoid impulse buying or buying items you already have in the cupboard or refrigerator.

- Make only half the recipe if you're experimenting with a dish or trying a new one. That way, you won't use a large amount of expensive ingredients on something that doesn't turn out the way you had hoped.

- Include one or two meatless meals in the weekly menu. Learn how to cook less expensive cuts of meat; reduce amount of meat used by preparing soups, salads, stews, and casseroles.

- Cook at home and from scratch whenever possible.

- Buy in-season fruits and vegetables.

- Take your own lunch and snacks to work with you. Pack lunches and snacks to eat while on car trips.

CLOTHES

- Use trendy scarves and inexpensive jewelry to update your wardrobe.

- Look for natural fibers. They tend to last longer and stay in style longer. Linen and wool are two natural fibers that show up season after season.

- Take care of your clothes by hanging them or folding them after each use, and following washing instructions.

- Steer clear of short-lived clothing fads. Even if the garment looks great on you, you're not going to want to wear it next year.

- Shop end-of-season sales. Look for high-quality clothes that have been marked down considerably.

- Mix and match clothes by investing in separates; resist the urge to buy a garment that coordinates with nothing else in your wardrobe.

- Focus on style, quality, and fit instead of quantity. You'll not only save money, but you'll feel confident about wearing anything in your closet.

ENTERTAINMENT

- Check your Chamber of Commerce website, library, or local newspaper for lists of free events and attractions. You're likely to discover farmer's markets, art shows, craft fairs, community concerts, and art exhibits.

- Share a magazine subscription with a neighbor, friend, or family member.

- Borrow books, CDs, and DVDs from the library instead of buying them.

- Browse used book stores for book bargains. Many take your used books in exchange.

- Go to movie matinees—tickets are almost always cheaper than during the evening hours. Where permitted, bring your own snacks.

- Cancel TV and movie services that you rarely or never use.

- Compare prices and book vacations ahead to get the best deals on airfare and hotels.

- Invite friends over for a potluck meal or cookout instead of an expensive sit-down dinner.

- Play cards and board games at home rather than going out.

SHOPPING

BUY SECOND HAND
Look for used items you need for the home rather than buying brand new. While obviously some things we want to purchase new, buying secondhand can save loads of money. Often older things are made better than the newer things today, making it an even better bargain for your money.

CONSOLIDATE CLEANING SUPPLIES
Instead of having a cleaner for this and a cleaner for that, try consolidating. Plain soap, baking soda, and vinegar will clean a lot. Generic window cleaner works fine, and generic disinfectant wipes work just as well as the name brand.

USE CLOTH DIAPERS
Save the disposable diapers for traveling and shopping and perhaps for sleeping time. Cloth diapers are not only better for baby's bottom, they save a lot of money because they are washable and reusable.

BUY GENERIC PRODUCTS
Does it really matter whether your milk or butter is made by an expensively advertised brand or is the store brand ok? Find what works for you and switch to generic brands for at least a part of your grocery list.

SHOPPING

AVOID IMPULSE BUYING
If you wait a day or two, you'll be able to check prices and make an informed decision to buy it at the best price.

SAVE WITH SECURITY
In some states, you can save money on your home and auto insurance if you have security options. For instance, if you have a fire extinguisher or alarm system, you may be eligible for an extra insurance discount. Call and check with your agent.

RARE LUXURIES
Sometimes you just need that certain little luxury. But, if you cut down on high-dollar indulgences and treat yourself to them less often, it makes them a real treat to be savored. So, indulge yourself with a spa treatment, a four-star restaurant, or even a single serving of your favorite, oh-so-expensive chocolate. Make it special by doing it very infrequently.

FOLLOW UP ON REBATES
After you buy a product with a rebate, send in the form immediately. Then mark your calendar to remind yourself to follow up with the rebate company if the check hasn't shown up.

SHOPPING

YARD SALES AND AUCTIONS

Great buys are happening in your neighborhood all the time, at local yard and garage sales, and auctions. Check the local classifieds for notices of estate sales and auctions. Other sources of information about local sales are all over the internet.

PRICE CHECK

For items that are expensive, do a price check before buying. Online coupons make it even easier to save some money. And, there are lots of online sites that specialize in comparison pricing.

AROUND THE HOUSE

- Swap jobs with neighbors. For example, you might babysit their kids in exchange for a few home-cooked meals, or a session of yard work.

- Unplug chargers and appliances, and switch off lights and fans when not in use.

- Install a programmable thermostat to control your air conditioning and heat usage.

- Put insulation around drafty windows.

- Invest in a solar water heater.

- Wash clothes in cold water using a cold-water detergent.

- Use cheap, plain white dishtowels instead of paper towels for wipe-ups. They can be washed with bleach in the washer.

- Change furnace filter regularly; have furnace checked regularly for efficient operation.

- Make as many home repairs as you can rather than pay someone to do them for you.

TRANSPORTATION AND TRAVEL

- Drive only when necessary. Walk, ride a bike, carpool, or take public transportation.

- Increase gas mileage by driving at a steady speed. Avoid a series of speed-ups and slowdowns; use cruise control when traveling long distances on the highway.

- Don't speed. It will save gas—and the cost of a speeding ticket!

- Turn off the engine rather than let it idle for long periods of time.

- Use the car's ventilation system instead of air conditioning when possible.

- Buy regular-grade gas unless your vehicle owner's manual specifies high octane fuel.

- Keep car well-maintained; check air tire pressure often and correct when necessary.

- Educate yourself before heading into a repair shop. Check the shop's reputation; get clear and detailed estimates for expensive jobs; get second or third estimates for the same work.

TRANSPORTATION AND TRAVEL

- Keep your car for as long as you can. Resist the temptation to trade in simply to have a new model.

- Buy a car based on your specific needs, driving conditions, and miles driven per year.

- Work from home at least part of the time if you can.

- Explore the feasibility of getting to your travel destination by bus or train rather than by air.

- Reduce luggage to only what you'll need to avoid baggage fees.

- Avoid peak travel days and dates whenever possible.

- Check in with a city's convention and visitor's bureau, where you may find discount coupons and attraction passes.

- Get foreign currency from your local bank rather than at an airport exchange kiosk.

- Research your destination at the library or online to pinpoint particular sites you want to visit and tours you want to take. You don't want to waste time or money on getting lost or feeling disappointed because a site wasn't what you had expected.

Don't Throw It Away—
REPURPOSE IT!

- Shred used wrapping paper for use as gift bag filler.

- Smooth used wrapping paper for use as drawer liners.

- Use a muffin tin, cupcake tray, egg carton, or baby food jars on the desk or worktable for small tools, beads, clips, and other tiny items.

- Use a muffin tin, cupcake tray, egg carton, or baby food jars to sort small jigsaw pieces by color or shape.

- Store electrical cords in empty wrapping paper tubes and paper towel tubes to keep them from tangling; run multiple cords through tubes to keep them neat when in use.

- Add shower hooks to hanger rods in closets for totes and purses.

- Remove the top of an old suitcase and place a soft cushion inside for a bed for a cat or small dog.

- Hang a see-through pocket-style shoe organizer in the pantry to hold kids' snack packs; in a hall closet for gloves and mittens; in the sewing or craft room for tools and fabric scraps.

Don't Throw It Away—
REPURPOSE IT!

- Use a six-bottle beverage carrier as a condiment holder.

- Turn an old colander or sieve into an outdoor planter.

- Mount a wire spice rack on the wall of the family room or kids' room to hold cell phone, remote, and other easily misplaced items.

- Put an old kitchen flatware holder in a dresser or bureau drawer to hold jewelry and other small items; in desk drawer for pens, clips, rubber bands.

- Nail empty food cans or decorative tins to the garage wall to hold garden snips, gloves, and other small tools.

- Use a gallon or half-gallon milk jug for watering potted plants.

- Those small drawstring gauze bags often used as gift bags for jewelry make excellent sachets. Simply add a teaspoonful of potpourri and tie!

THRIFTY LIVING

DAILY EXPENSES ADD UP
In a small notebook, keep track of how much money you spend each day. List everything, even small purchases. At the end of the week, you may be surprised to realize how much money has slipped through your fingers on beverages, snacks, or lottery tickets. If you could cut $3 a day out of your nonessential spending, you could save nearly $100 every month!

PAY YOURSELF FIRST
Have a set amount of your income directed from your paycheck to your savings or 401k. If you don't see it, you can't spend it.

FIND JOY IN SAVING
A lot of people find joy in spending money. But, you can blaze your own trail – make it your favorite thing to do to find ways to keep your money.

TUNE OUT THE ADS
Ads are about wants – wanting things you don't have, being dissatisfied with the things you do have. Tune them out, and tune into what you enjoy. Be content with what you have: contentment begins when comparison stops.

THRIFTY LIVING

KEEP TRACK OF YOUR CASH
Keep a record of where your money goes, by keeping a
diary or a spending journal. If you are conscious of your
spending you've taken the first step to controlling
your budget and saving for the future.

**LOOK AT THE LITTLE THINGS YOU SPEND
YOUR MONEY ON EVERY DAY**
Redirect that spending to yourself. Put aside a few dollars
a day for your future rather than spending it on little
purchases such as lattés, fancy coffees, bottled water, fast
food, cigarettes, magazines and snacks. It adds up.

PAY OFF DEBT
If you carry any debt, focus on consolidating it to a lower
interest and paying it off as soon as possible. Start with
one debt at a time, and focus on paying it off, then move
on to the next one. Money paid in interest is money
thrown away!

BE THANKFUL
One of the best ways to save for the future is to be content
with what you have. In fact, give thanks for all the bless-
ings you have – your life, your health, your family and
friends. Be content. It is enough.

THRIFTY LIVING

BUY SLOWLY
When considering any major purchase, wait. Pausing before we purchase can keep us from buying on a whim. Impulse buying is one of the causes of credit card debt in our country. Credit cards give us an illusionary buying power. At least wait overnight – better yet, wait a week to decide. It'll still be there, and you'll make a calm, reasoned decision.

READ MORE
Reading is one of the cheapest – and most beneficial – hobbies around. Most towns have a library available to the public – just go there and check out some books that interest you. Then, spend some of your free time reading in a cozy place in your house.

DAILY INSPIRATION
Perhaps you're inspired to make changes by your children, your spouse, or a friend or family member. Maybe it's a personal goal, like early retirement. Find something that makes you want to save; use that inspiration as a constant reminder.

THRIFTY LIVING

SAY GOODBYE TO LATE FEES
Get your regular bills organized. If possible, pay online to automate payments. If your bill is due before your paycheck arrives, call the creditor and ask to have the due date changed.

AVOID OVERDRAFT FEES
If you use your checking account often or have some bills that are paid automatically from your checking account, be aware of the balance and avoid overdraft fees.

DUMP ATM FEES
Be aware of the ATM withdrawal fees charged by your bank. Be sure to use only those ATM machines where your bank will not charge the fees, or withdraw directly at your bank.

GET RID OF ANNUAL FEES
Credit cards with their cash back bonuses and reward points are a great way to save some money. Lots of cards offer fee-free reward plans, so there really is no reason to pay annual fees.

CHAPTER 5

Celebrations, Holidays, and Gifts Made Easy!

Special times mean special celebrations. Far too often, however, we get to the "big day" and find we're so worn out with all the preparations that we can't enjoy the event itself! And then come the bills—whew!

In this section, you will find ways to simplify celebrations without sacrificing warmth, hospitality, and fun. These pages are crammed with inventive ideas for center-pieces, snacks, appetizers, and gifts that are easily put together and sure to please. What's more, many call for nothing more than items you probably have on hand right now!

Here's how to make your celebrations easy on your pocketbook and easy on you

Easy-to-Make
FUN AND FESTIVE FOODS
for Any Occasion

- Take a flour tortilla and use cookie cutters to cut out fun shapes. Arrange shapes on a cookie sheet and spray lightly with cooking spray. Bake at 350° until crispy (about 5 minutes).

- Add pick-up appeal to your next tray of cheese cubes by replacing toothpicks with thin pretzel sticks.

- Turn a dish of vanilla pudding into a festive dessert by sprinkling the top with fruit-flavored gelatin crystals.

- Freeze sprigs of mint in ice cubes to use in tea; bits of orange or pineapple for coolers; slice of lemon for lemonade.

- Shape refrigerator biscuit dough into letters spelling out the guest of honor's name, the occasion, or message of your choice. Brush with melted butter; add sesame seeds, cinnamon and sugar, or grated cheese, if desired; bake.

- Use cookie cutters to make any desired sandwich shape for your occasion.

Easy-to-Make
FUN AND FESTIVE FOODS
for Any Occasion

- Create an eye-catching springtime appetizer! You'll need about 18 fresh Chinese snow peas and about 2 cups of your favorite tuna, chicken, crab, or ham spread. Steam peas or blanche in water for 30 seconds until slightly softened. Drain and dunk in ice water. Drain and lay out to dry. Meanwhile, prepare spread with desired seasonings. With a sharp knife, split each pea pod at the top seam. Fill with 1 tablespoon of spread. Place side by side on serving dish. If not serving immediately, cover and refrigerate.

- Make mini ice cream sandwiches with a spoonful of ice cream, fruit sorbet, or yogurt between two vanilla wafers. Freeze until ready to serve.

- Wash cherry tomatoes and slice off tops. Scoop out pulp and fill with a creamy cheese dip, guacamole, or hummus.

- Add food coloring to cake or cupcake batter to fit the occasion.

- Dip washed and dried mint leaves in melted chocolate. Place on wax paper and cool until firm; refrigerate leaves until ready to use as a garnish with berries or on dessert plates.

HARVEST OF HINTS

- After the frost, collect a few interesting branches and gather them together with raffia or twine. Hang from wall or door, branches facing up, and insert your favorite photos into the branches.

- Visit your local farmer's market for the best selection of fall's bounty. You'll be supporting your community and saving money too.

- Fill a large cylinder-shaped vase with miniature pumpkins and gourds for a long-lasting centerpiece.

- Enjoy a fall day by taking a walk and collecting beautiful leaves. Place the leaves between sheets of wax paper, cover with a towel, and press with a medium iron (no steam) to seal the wax paper sheets together. Flip and repeat to seal other side. Cut around leaves, leaving a small margin of wax paper around the edge.

- Hot-glue preserved leaves and acorns around the rim of an old straw hat. Add a colorful orange ribbon, and hang it on your front door instead of a wreath.

HARVEST OF HINTS

- Make tasty little "haystack" treats by stirring thin chow mein noodles into melted butterscotch chips. Drop on wax paper and add a little pumpkin-shaped candy at the base before cooling in the refrigerator.

- Start a fun family tradition by taking the whole family to a corn maze. They'll look forward to doing it every year!

- Host a pot-luck party, asking contributors to bring a fall-themed dish. Attach your invitation to a pressed, colorful leaf.

- Cut an opening in an apple and insert a votive candle.

- Create a plate stand by gluing a terra cotta plant draining platter to an inverted terra cotta pot. Use it to display gourds, nuts and miniature pumpkins, or a pumpkin bundt cake.

- Roasted root vegetables are an easy fall meal. Drizzle olive oil over beets, carrots, parsnips, onions, potatoes and your favorite veggies in a cake pan. Season and bake at 350 degrees until tender.

HARVEST OF HINTS

- Collect different sizes of stemmed glassware. Place a flameless LED tea light candle under inverted glass. Place a miniature pumpkin on top (formerly the base) of the glass. Tie raffia around the stem and arrange for a colorful harvest centerpiece.

- Make a welcoming front-door arrangement by filling an old wheelbarrow with pumpkins, squash, gourds and vines.

- Kale is plentiful this time of year and makes a delicious snack chip. Simply remove washed and dried leaves from the stems, drizzle leaves with olive oil and sea salt and bake at 350 degrees until edges are brown (about 10 minutes).

- Your home will smell like a heavenly fall day when you simmer some cinnamon sticks, cloves and nutmeg in a pot of water on top of your stove.

- Fill antique canning jars with colorful seasonal finds (berries, acorns, dried beans, candy corn, nuts, colorful leaves etc). Tie with burlap or fall ribbon and place throughout the home for a homespun touch.

Holiday Entertaining– Fall/Thanksgiving
HARVEST OF HINTS

- Using real leaves as templates, cut leaf shapes out of felt. Glue leaves onto inexpensive pillows and place-mats to use throughout the season.

- Hollow out pumpkins and place colorful blooming mums inside. Line them up around the walkway to your home.

Holiday Entertaining– Fall/Thanksgiving
THANKSGIVING COOKING

- Organization is the key! Many dishes can be made a week ahead of time and frozen. Do as much shopping as you can weeks ahead so you can spread out the grocery payments. Use coupons!

- The day before: chop onion and celery and herbs for the dressing, and measure out seasoning so all you need to do is add it to the dried bread.

- Use bagged, pre-washed lettuce if serving salad.

THANKSGIVING COOKING

- Instead of peeling and mashing, boil unpeeled, scrubbed new potatoes and serve in chunks, letting guests add their own toppings such as sour cream, butter and spices. Leftovers can be fried, or cubed and added to soups or casseroles.

- Bake whole yams and serve halved with brown sugar, butter and maple syrup.

- Don't be afraid to accept help! Put children to work setting the table. Ask friends to handle beverage service while you put the finishing touches on the meal.

- Keep half the sink full of hot soapy water so you can take care of dishes as you work.

- Remember, frozen turkey takes 3-5 days to thaw in the refrigerator. Plan accordingly!

- The day before, plan a picnic. Spread a blanket on the family room floor and let your family eat off paper plates. Then you can set the table for the Thanksgiving meal early.

THANKSGIVING COOKING

- Start a new tradition. Buy an inexpensive white table cloth. During dinner, have guests sign the tablecloth with permanent fabric markers. Through the years it will be a fun reminder of the holiday celebrations. If you are craft-minded, you can embroider over the signatures to create an heirloom.

- Using smaller dinner plates will help reduce food waste with children, who often fill their plates and then just eat a bite.

- Line the trash can with three bags. As the filled one is removed, another will be ready to go.

- Heavily shake table salt on new oven spills. Wipe up with damp sponge or paper towel once the oven cools.

- Simplify cleanup by using a disposable roasting pan. Watch for sales in the weeks before the holiday.

- Take advantage of the supermarket deli. Basics like cranberry sauce and simple salads can be doctored up with a garnish, such as an orange twist, fresh parsley or thyme.

THANKSGIVING COOKING

- Keep children busy before the meal by having them cut leaf shapes out of construction paper. Before dinner, have everyone take a leaf and write down what they are thankful for and place leaves in a decorative bowl to use as a centerpiece.

- Place marked bins by the door to make it easy for guests to recycle, saving you sorting and cleanup time later.

- Keep a 3-ring Thanksgiving binder where you store notes, recipes, pictures and hints from year to year.

- When all is said and done, and tummies are full, invite a conversation around the table asking all to name something they are thankful for. Your guests will leave feeling happy and positive.

ENTERTAINING HOLIDAYS

- Core red apples and insert candles of various heights for the table and kitchen counter.

- Tie each napkin with ribbon or gold cord, and then tuck a candy cane in the bow. Attach a gift tag with guest's name.

- Flavor punch with orange slices ringed with cloves.

- Tie a ribbon with a miniature ornament attached around serving bowls, the bread basket, or use as napkin rings.

- Decorate dessert plates by sprinkling cocoa, cinnamon, or powdered sugar onto plate through a cooling rack.

- Place sprigs of greenery around serving platters. Put a votive candle in the middle of platters for appetizers and other finger food.

- Slice apples widthwise. Then cut out the core with a miniature cookie cutter. Add to punch bowls, or arrange on fruit plate.

ENTERTAINING HOLIDAYS

- Mix and freeze unbaked, undecorated cookie dough before the holidays. Thaw, decorate, and bake as needed for quick and convenient entertaining and gift-giving.

- Cut biscuit dough with Christmas cookie cutters for a festive holiday brunch. Serve with a selection of flavored butters.

- Tie different colors of thin ribbon around the stems of stemmed glassware, each with a different miniature ornament attached so guests can identify which glass is theirs.

- Make an edible bowl for treats by lining a small bowl with aluminum foil. Pipe melted chocolate in a lacy design inside the bowl, then refrigerate. When completely firm, remove the foil and carefully peel away from the chocolate. Refrigerate until serving time then fill with berries or sweets.

- Serve ice cream and similar desserts in festive stemmed glassware. Hang a miniature candy cane over the rim, or top ice cream with a chocolate kiss.

ENTERTAINING HOLIDAYS

- Create a Christmas tree cake by cutting a rectangle from a square cake. Cut rectangle diagonally and arrange into a triangle. Cut remaining slice into squares for tree trunk and presents; use colored frosting, sprinkles, and gumdrops to decorate; top with a star-shaped sugar cookie.

- Dress up your table by laying a Christmas wreath in the middle and placing a pretty serving bowl in its center.

- On an appetizer tray, alternate white cheese cubes and cherry tomatoes in strips to form a Christmas tree, candy cane or Christmas stocking. Surround with crackers to feature the shape.

- Stack cookies, wrap in a bundle with clear wrap and tie closed with ribbon. If desired, insert stack in a tall clear drinking glass, jar, or vase to give as gifts.

- Use holiday place cards to identify different cheeses on the cheese tray, or to list the ingredients of main dishes on a buffet table. Note if dish is vegetarian, gluten-free or contains nuts.

A CHOCOLATE LOVER'S CHRISTMAS

*NOTE: Chocolate's worst enemies are
overcooking and water moisture.*

- Drizzle melted chocolate across desserts and dessert plates by placing chocolate in a small resealable plastic bag; seal, then snip one corner to form a tiny opening. *Note: Be sure chocolate is not so hot that it would melt bag.*

- Add chocolate morsels to nut, date, banana, or pumpkin muffin, bread, and coffee cake recipes.

- Add chocolate morsels to pancake and waffle mix for a sweet breakfast or brunch.

- Combine 3 parts instant cocoa mix and 1 part instant coffee; add boiling water, plus whipped cream or marshmallows if desired, for a quick pick-me-up cup of cocoa-coffee.

- Make chocolate curls by pouring a smooth, level layer of melted chocolate onto a wax paper lined cookie sheet; cool; then pull a vegetable peeler across layer. Refrigerate curls until ready to serve as a topping or garnish.

A CHOCOLATE LOVER'S CHRISTMAS

- Dip the bottom half of peppermint sticks into melted chocolate and place on wax paper. Chill until firm.

- Grate chocolate in a food processor, or grate by hand using wax paper to hold the chocolate so heat from your hand will not melt the chunk. Sprinkle grated chocolate over ice cream, whipped cream, cookies, and eggnog.

- Give a selection of homemade fudge, brownies, cocoa mix, chocolate bark, and chocolate cookies as gifts. Pack in decorative basket, jar, box or tin.

- Make chocolate "stirring spoons" by dipping small plastic heat-resistant spoons into melted white or dark chocolate. Place on wax paper; add sprinkles if desired. Chill until chocolate is firm.

- Attach wrapped chocolates to a hallway wreath or table-top tree; allow visiting kids to pick a piece to take home as a special treat.

- Add chocolate morsels or chunks to snack mixes and nuts for a quick and easy crowd-pleaser.

A CHOCOLATE LOVER'S CHRISTMAS

- Serve a chocolate spoon or peppermint stick as a stirrer with a cup of hot chocolate or eggnog.

- Pipe chocolate squiggles onto graham crackers to please young guests.

- Crumble a white or dark chocolate bar into a cup of steaming milk for a rich and flavorful drink. Add whipped cream, chocolate drizzles, peppermint or cinnamon stick if desired.

- Make chocolate shapes by pouring a smooth, level layer of melted chocolate onto a wax-paper lined cookie sheet. Chill slightly, then cut shapes with cookie cutter. Garnish if desired. When chocolate is firm, carefully lift shapes out. Refrigerate until ready to use.

- Make a chocolate sled by placing a wrapped chocolate bar on two candy cane "runners." Attach with a small square of tape on the underside. Load the sled with a stock of individually wrapped chocolate candies.

TREATS & SNACKS

- Create a "Christmas tree" by arranging celery sticks, cut in pairs of increasing length as branches. Place cherry tomatoes as ornaments. Cut a slice of yellow bell pepper for a star at the top of the tree.

- Slide bite-sized chunks of pineapple, honeydew, star fruit or kiwi fruit slices, red and green grapes, strawberries or cherries on bamboo skewers for colorful fruit kabobs.

- Make festive pasta kabobs with cooked tortellini, cherry tomatoes, and chunks of mozzarella cheese. Add a dip if desired.

- Top whipped cream and ice cream with a small, shaped Christmas cookie or colorful candies.

- Add red or green food coloring to water to make colorful ice cubes for ice buckets.

- Stack bite-sized brownies on a cake stand to form a tiered Christmas tree. Decorate with gold or green piped frosting, color-coated candies, candied fruit, peppermints, and gumdrops. Top with a star-shaped sugar cookie.

TREATS & SNACKS

- Slice cucumbers in half lengthwise and scoop out most of the centers to form "boats." Fill each with chutney, cream cheese, or other filling. Slice into 1/2" pieces and top each piece with a parsley sprig, or piece of cherry tomato or red pepper.

- Make pigs in a blanket by rolling cocktail-sized wieners into mini crescent rolls. Add cheese and bacon if desired. Bake. Serve with tangy dipping sauce.

- Sprinkle crushed candy canes over frosting, whipped cream, or ice cream.

- Dice red, green, and yellow peppers. Add to the top of cheese spreads and dips, or sprinkle over nachos.

- Set up an old-fashioned candy store the kids will go running to. Arrange several glass canisters and old-fashioned jars on a low table. Fill them with a variety of colorful candies. Keep resealable snack bags on the table, so kids can fill snack bags with desired candies.

TREATS & SNACKS

- Top chocolate or white mini cupcakes with a layer of whipped cream, a strawberry, and a tiny "pom-pom" of whipped cream for cute Santa-hat bites.

- Make the cheese and cracker tray festive by garnishing it with star fruit, cherry tomatoes, and mint leaves.

- For a fluffy dip to serve with fruit, beat together 8 oz. cream cheese, 1/2 c. light corn syrup, 1/3 c. brown sugar, 1/4 c. peanut butter and 1 tsp. vanilla. Refrigerate.

- Use hollowed apples for serving the fluffy fruit dip above or a melted chocolate dip or other dip. Surround with strawberries, apples, pears, orange slices, marshmallows and pound cake bites.

- Layer red and green color-coated candies in small, clear glass jars. Tie with a ribbon and attach a gift tag with guest's name. Use as a place card at the dining room table, plus a take-home treat after the party.

TREATS & SNACKS

- Stir-fry thin strips of chicken. Slide strips on bamboo skewers and serve with teriyaki, peanut, or soy dipping sauce.

- Put nuts, small candies, and snack mix in festive paper muffin cups for quick and convenient individual servings.

- Place chunks of chocolate on top of waffle pretzels. Bake for about 5 minutes at about 300 degrees, then cool. Top with sprinkles.

- Serve a scoop of vanilla ice cream along with a selection of add-your-own toppings, such as color-coated candies, chocolate morsels, cookie crumbles, nuts, chopped strawberries. Add whipped cream.

GIFTY KITCHEN IDEAS

- Take a photo of yourself (and helpers) in the process of creating the homemade gift. Use the photo as your gift tag.

- To make gift tags for homemade cookies, trace around a cookie cutter and cut out.

- Wrap a holiday hand towel, tea towel, cloth napkin, or length of fabric around gifts of food and beverage. Secure with a colorful ribbon.

- Freeze portions of favorite main dishes and soups in microwaveable plastic containers. Use a Christmas sticker to label contents. Deliver to seniors, singles, and college students so they have tasty homemade meals in their freezer.

- Bundle cinnamon sticks, candy canes, peppermint sticks, or pretzel rods together. Tie with colored ribbon and attach to homemade food item.

- Create a "coupon book" for the busy mom or house-bound friend. Offer to make and deliver several specific dishes or desserts upon request.

GIFTY KITCHEN IDEAS

- Choose a selection of teas or coffees. Arrange in a basket along with your choice of items: teacup and teapot, or coffee mug; biscuits, wafers, or shortbread cookies. Add a package of holiday napkins.

- Create an ice cream lover's delight with a basket containing ice cream cones or sundae cups, ice cream scoop, jarred toppings and syrup, packets of nuts, candies, chocolate morsels, sprinkles. Let the happy recipient supply the ice cream!

- Make plain cookie dough, then freeze it. Put it in gift basket along with a selection of decorations, such as sprinkles in various colors, sugar, chocolate beads, gumdrops. Add baking directions, along with a note to keep dough frozen until ready to use.

- Create fun packaging for foodies' gifts by adding a kitchen item, such as wooden spoons, kitchen timer, cookie cutters, whisk, holiday napkins, ice cream scoop, novelty cheese cutter, decorative coasters, gourmet sea salt, cooks' non-scented hand lotion

GIFTY KITCHEN IDEAS

- Select packets of herb seeds. Combine in a basket with small flower pots, tiny trowel, and potting mix.

- Sew a border of red and green ribbons or Christmas cotton print to the bottom of a red or green kitchen hand towel for a one-of-a-kind gift.

- Make or buy holiday-themed pot holders or oven mitts and give with a food gift or kitchen utensil or appliance.

- Put together a collection of soup and chili mixes with one or two soup bowls and crackers. Add garnishes if desired. Attach a soup spoon.

- Create in-the-jar gifts with cocoa mix, cake, bread and cookie mix or pancake and waffle mix or gumdrops, granola and snack mixes or jam, jelly and chutney.

- Make an edible centerpiece for the appetizer table by stacking bite-sized pieces of fruits or vegetables on bamboo skewers. Arrange as a bouquet in an upturned head of cabbage and set in a bowl. Hide cabbage with crackers or chips. Provide dips.

GIFTY KITCHEN IDEAS

- Fill a colander with a selection of pastas, garlic bread sticks, Parmesan cheese, and a jar of homemade pasta sauce. Wrap in cellophane and tie with a colorful bow.

- Create a gift for salad lovers by filling a wooden bowl with croutons, chips, bacon bits, almonds, canned artichoke hearts and hearts of palm, a pepper mill, and a selection of salad dressings.

- Make homemade soup and pour into a securely sealed jar. Freeze or refrigerate until ready to gift. Add fun bowl, napkins, or tea towel.

- Stack homemade fudge on a decorative kitchen tile, small butcher block or cutting board. Wrap with cellophane and tie with a colorful ribbon.

Weddings, Showers, and Anniversaries
FUN AND EASY BRIDAL OR BABY SHOWER FAVORS

- Instead of buying small boxes, wrap favors in swatches of themed fabric tied with a bow.

- Shop dollar stores for small, yet useful, items that would make fun favors: die-cut note paper, journals, pens, sachets, aromatic candles, novelty soaps, hand or body lotion.

- Homemade cookies and brownies, small loaf cakes, snack mix, cupcakes, or novelty chocolates make tasty favors!

- If you have a flower garden, something as simple as a bud or blossom in a tube stem holder tied with a ribbon makes a lovely favor.

- Gather an assortment of small, decorative teacups at garage sales. Use as planters for herbs or succulents; containers for pincushions or candles (instructions can be found on Internet sewing and craft sites); holders for tiny plush puppies, kittens, or any other cute critter.

- Create bookmarks from designed paper or greeting cards, and add a serious, inspirational, or humorous quote that speaks to the occasion.

- Cut gauzy fabric into squares. Put a handful of chocolate candies in the middle; draw up the edges and tie with ribbon.

GIFTS FOR WEDDING/ANNIVERSARY

Anniversary	*Traditional*	*Modern*
First	Paper	Clocks
Second	Cotton	China
Third	Leather	Crystal, Glass
Fourth	Linen	Appliances
Fifth	Wood	Silverware
Sixth	Iron	Wood
Seventh	Wool	Desk Sets
Eighth	Bronze	Linen, Lace
Ninth	Pottery	Leather
Tenth	Tin, Aluminum	Diamond Jewelry
Eleventh	Steel	Fashion Jewelry

GIFTS FOR WEDDING/ANNIVERSARY

Anniversary	Traditional	Modern
Twelfth	Silk	Pearls, Colored Gems
Thirteenth	Lace	Textiles, Furs
Fourteenth	Ivory	Gold Jewelry
Fifteenth	Crystal	Watches
Twentieth	China	Platinum
Twenty-fifth	Silver	Sterling Silver
Thirtieth	Pearl	Diamond
Thirty-fifth	Coral, Jade	Jade
Fortieth	Ruby	Ruby
Forty-fifth	Sapphire	Sapphire
Fiftieth	Gold	Gold
Fifty-fifth	Emerald	Emerald
Sixtieth	Diamond	Diamond

BIRTHSTONES AND FLOWERS

JANUARY
Garnet
Carnation or Snowdrop

FEBRUARY
Amethyst
Violet or Primrose

MARCH
Bloodstone or Aquamarine
Jonquil or Daffodil

APRIL
Diamond
Sweet Pea or Daisy

MAY
Emerald
Lily of the Valley or Hawthorne

JUNE
Pearl or Alexandrite
Rose or Honeysuckle

JULY
Ruby
Larkspur or Water Lily

AUGUST
Sardonyx or Peridot
Poppy or Gladiolus

SEPTEMBER
Sapphire
Aster or Morning Glory

OCTOBER
Opal or Tourmaline
Calendula or Cosmos

NOVEMBER
Topaz
Chrysanthemum

DECEMBER
Turquoise or Zircon
Narcissus or Holly

Fun, Functional, and Oh-So-Appreciated
GIFT IDEAS

ENTERTAINMENT COUPON BOOK
A coupon book filled with local and national coupons
that can be used for movies, restaurants, sporting events,
travel, gasoline, and lots more. It makes a great gift and
literally keeps giving all year long because everyone loves
to save money.

MIXES IN A JAR
Easy to make and inexpensive. Just about anything can
be made in a jar: Milk Bath in a Jar, Hot Spiced Cider Mix,
Chocolate Chip Cookies, French Vanilla Cocoa Mix and dry
ingredients for soups. To make it personal, add your own
hangtag with cooking directions, and a fun fact or note
that connects with the recipient in a meaningful way.

THEME GIFT BASKETS
Inexpensive baskets can be found throughout the year at
garage sales and flea markets. The jar gifts above and many
other items can be added to the baskets. Be creative. Here
are just a few theme basket ideas:

Chocolate Lover – cookies, popcorn, a few very
special chocolates.
Golf Lover – tees, balls, towels, gift certificates.

Fun, Functional, and Oh-So-Appreciated
GIFT IDEAS

Coffee Lover – coffee beans, coffee flavorings, cappuccino mix, cups.
Spa Lover – homemade lotions & gels, perfume, salts, soaps.
Movie Lover – a DVD plus packs of popcorn and movie candy.

CARING COUPONS
Make a book of your own coupons, to provide services for various occasions: baby sitting for new parents, a back rub for a stressed-out spouse, cooking dinner for a friend, an ice cream after school for a student. Very inexpensive, these wonderfully thoughtful gifts will be cherished.

GIFT OF THE MONTH CLUB
Give someone the gift of Cookies of the month, Movie of the month, Coffee of the month, Flower of the month. You can make a coupon book or gift certificates.

PICTURE THIS
Find nice photos of you and your friend or relative together. Use an inexpensive frame to make it a nice presentation. There's nothing so personal as an image of you and your companion together.

Fun, Functional, and Oh-So-Appreciated
GIFT IDEAS

GIFT DRAWING
During the holidays, when everyone seems to be low on funds, suggest a gift swap drawing. This way each person doesn't have to buy for everyone, just one person. The names can be kept a secret, or made known (sometimes it's more fun to do it secretly). You can also set a price limit for the cost of the gifts.

GIFT ACCENTS
Add small items to package along with or instead of bows: candy canes, pine cones, chocolate kisses, cinnamon sticks, bells, sachets, beads, and mistletoe. Homemade printed gift tags with personal messages also add a special touch!

RECIPE BOOKS
A great personalized gift: Collect family food favorites, and make hand-written cards for a small recipe box, or create an album. Recipes can all be in one subject, like chocolate for the chocolate lover, vegetarian, or bread recipes. Or, they can just be the recipient's favorites.

Fun, Functional, and Oh-So-Appreciated
GIFT IDEAS

SPREAD OUT THE SPENDING
You can save money by buying a little at a time: buy gifts when they're on sale. Keep Christmas in mind, or other upcoming gift-giving occasions when you shop and see something that your best friend, family member, or coworker would like. With this tactic you don't have to scramble at the last minute, and, you don't end up spending so much money all at once.

CHAPTER 6

Important Checklists

When you have a lot to do, lists are essential. They relieve you of lingering worries that you have forgotten something or neglected to take care of an essential task. When you've check off an item, you know it's been done. Not only are these lists handy to have on-hand, they also serve as a convenient way to review important information with other members of the family.

This section opens with a list of Important Phone Numbers. Make sure everyone in the family knows where to find these numbers. Share them with babysitters, in-home caregivers, and anyone looking after your property when you're away. Keep the Location of Personal Papers list in your files; give a copy to a trusted family member or friend.

The Household Maintenance list provides an easy way for first-time as well as experienced homeowners to keep on top of routine home maintenance. And the Emergency Checklist is an invaluable guide for what everyone needs to have ready in case the unexpected happens. You will benefit, and so will those around you!

Important Checklists
PHONE NUMBERS

Here's a one-stop reference for important phone numbers. Even if you have them stored in your cellphone, a backup hard-copy list can come to the rescue if you misplace your phone or the phone loses data or power. For easy identification, circle or highlight ICE (In Case of Emergency) numbers. These may include doctors as well as neighbors or nearby relatives that family members in need should call.

- ☐ 911
- ☐ Poison Control
- ☐ Local Fire
- ☐ Local Police (Non-Emergency)
- ☐ Ambulance
- ☐ Emergency Room
- ☐ Hospital
- ☐ After hours Care
- ☐ Doctor's Office (Adults)
- ☐ Doctor's Office (Child)
- ☐ Dentist
- ☐ Pharmacy
- ☐ Health Insurance
- ☐ Car Insurance
- ☐ Home Insurance
- ☐ Credit Card Company
- ☐ Alarm Company
- ☐ Telephone Company
- ☐ Plumber
- ☐ Electrician

- ☐ Glass Repair
- ☐ Handyman
- ☐ Towing Company
- ☐ Taxi
- ☐ Locksmith
- ☐ Utility Company
- ☐ Sanitation Company
- ☐ Veterinarian
- ☐ Animal Control
- ☐ Neighbors
- ☐ School
- ☐ Daycare
- ☐ Babysitter
- ☐ Neighbors
- ☐ Relatives
- ☐ Co-workers
- ☐ Boss
- ☐ Library
- ☐ Bank
- ☐ Gym
- ☐ Take-out Food

IMPORTANT PERSONAL PAPERS

- ☐ **Birth Certificate**
- ☐ **Marriage Certificate**
- ☐ **Last Will and Testament**
  Power Of Attorny
  Executor
- ☐ **Living Will Information**
- ☐ **Insurance**
  Home
  Car
  Disability
  Long Term Care
- ☐ **Divorce Decree**
- ☐ **Military Records**
- ☐ **Naturalization Papers**
- ☐ **Organ Donor Information**
- ☐ **Social Security Card**
- ☐ **Trust Agreement**
- ☐ **Tax Returns**
  Tax Preparer

- ☐ **Post Office Box**
  Adress of Post Office,
  Owner of the P.O. Box
  Number of the Box, Key
  to the box location,
  Combination of the box
- ☐ **Safe Deposit Box**
  Bank, Address, Bank
  Phone #, The name
  on the box, The key
  location, The box
  contents

Important Checklists
HOUSEHOLD MAINTENACE

- ☐ Have fire extinguisher serviced
- ☐ Change batteries on answering machine
- ☐ Change batteries in smoke alarms, carbon monoxide detectors, and other safety alarms
- ☐ Remove dryer lint
- ☐ Clean stove hoods, room fans, heating & cooling vents
- ☐ Schedule seasonal maintenance on heating and cooling systems
- ☐ Change furnace filters
- ☐ With vacuum attachment, clean freezer & refrigerator coils
- ☐ Check hoses and seals on all appliances
- ☐ Clean or service fireplace for changing seasons
- ☐ Check window and door latches
- ☐ Check all faucets and under sinks for leaks
- ☐ Inspect crawl space and basement for leaks and dampness
- ☐ Clean gutters
- ☐ Inspect windows and screens, and change out for season
- ☐ Check air leaks and weather-strip for season
- ☐ Look for critter access through fireplace, attic, foundation, etc and seal
- ☐ Drain water from outdoor hoses, and store hoses for cold weather

Important Checklists
SPRING CLEANING

We call it spring cleaning, but here's a really helpful tip: don't reserve all your cleaning tasks for spring! It's way too easy to get distracted by the beautiful days and the desire to play and relax outdoors! Just be sure you can check off that these tasks have been accomplished AT LEAST once during the year.

☐ Clean matress covers, shams, and pillows
☐ Wash windows and window screens
☐ Wash ceilings and walls
☐ Dust and clean blinds
☐ Clean ceiling fan blades
☐ Clean the top and sides of doors
☐ Shampoo carpets and wax floors
☐ Clean lampshades
☐ Dust and clean light fixtures
☐ Clean doorknobs, drawer handles, etc.
☐ Wipe down handrails
☐ Oil door hinges
☐ Clean under furniture and heavy appliances such as the frigerator, oven, washing machine, dryer, etc.
☐ Clean dryer vent
☐ Reseal grout and repair caulking
☐ Clean window treatments

- ☐ Clean and polish jewelry, silver, brass, and copper
- ☐ Wax wood furniture
- ☐ Clean backsplash and kitchen walls
- ☐ Clean oven, cupboards, and hard to reach cabinets
- ☐ Empty the pantry, clean and reorganize
- ☐ Organize coat closets and store winter jackets
- ☐ Clean swithplates throughout the house
- ☐ Clean vent covers or other furnace outlet grates
- ☐ Empty vanities, clean and reorganize
- ☐ Sharpen knives
- ☐ Wash and sanitize all the cutting boards
- ☐ Shine silverware and other fancy dishes etc.
- ☐ Wash table linens and napkins
- ☐ Clean table legs and other hard to reach parts of furniture
- ☐ Dust picture frames and decorative wall hangings
- ☐ Launder decorative pillows and blankets
- ☐ Clean TV with a microfiber cloth
- ☐ Dust electronics (stereo, computer, etc.)
- ☐ Tidy up TV, stereo, and computer cables
- ☐ Organize DVD and music
- ☐ Purge home office files
- ☐ Organize computer files
- ☐ Backup computer files
- ☐ Sweep walkways, porches, decks, etc.
- ☐ Empty bookcases, clean and reorganize

EMERGENCY CHECKLIST

- ☐ Important documents, insurance, medical records, bank and financial info, Social Security cards, birth certificates, tax returns, etc. Keep in waterproof container.
- ☐ Water–1 gallon per day for each person
- ☐ Food–Non-perishables, canned food, peanut butter, energy bars, dried fruit
- ☐ Flashlight and batteries
- ☐ Battery-powered or emergency radio
- ☐ First Aid Kit
- ☐ Medications and other medical needs
- ☐ Eyeglasses
- ☐ Personal hygiene and sanitary products
- ☐ Multi-purpose tool or knife
- ☐ Cell phones–fully charged, with charger and extra batteries
- ☐ Cash and credit cards– in case banks and ATMs are not available
- ☐ Extra clothing–seasonal gear, comfortable heavy duty shoes
- ☐ Blankets and pillows
- ☐ Purse/Wallet with driver's license
- ☐ Fire extinguisher
- ☐ Laptop computer